Quick Guide to L

This guide is organized by families so related species are shown together. The Species Account pages are colour-coded and thumb-indexed in the following manner:

Waterfowl (Geese, Swans, Dabbling Ducks, Diving Ducks)

Upland Game Birds (Pheasant, Grouse, Quail)—Loons—Grebes—Cormorants—Wading Birds (Bittern, Heron)

Vulture—Diurnal Raptors (Eagles, Hawks, Falcons)

Rail and Coot—Shorebirds (Plovers, Sandpipers, Curlew, Dowitchers, Snipe, Phalaropes)

Gulls and Terns

Pigeons and Doves—Owls—Nighthawk—Poorwill—Swifts

Hummingbirds—Kingfisher—Woodpeckers—Flycatchers (Wood-Pewee, Flycatchers, Phoebe, Kingbirds)

Shrike—Vireos—Corvids (Jays, Crow, Raven)—Swallows

Chickadees—Nuthatches—Creeper—Wrens—Dipper—Kinglets—Thrushes (Bluebirds, Solitaire, Thrushes, Robin)

Catbird—Thrasher—Starling—Pipit—Waxwing—Warblers—Tanager

Native Sparrows (Towhee, Sparrows, Junco, Longspur, Snow Bunting)—Black-headed Grosbeak, Lazuli Bunting

Blackbirds (Bobolink, Blackbirds, Meadowlark, Cowbird, Oriole)—Finches (Finches, Pine Grosbeak, Crossbills, Siskin, Evening Grosbeak)—House Sparrow

Also by Richard Cannings

Roadside Nature Tours through the Okanagan: A Guide to British Columbia's Wine Country, Greystone Books, 2009.

Spotted Owls: Shadows in an Old-Growth Forest, Greystone Books, 2007.

An Enchantment of Birds, Greystone Books, 2007.

The Rockies: A Natural History, Greystone Books, 2005.

Birds of Southwestern British Columbia, with Tom Aversa and Hal Opperman, Heritage House, 2005.

British Columbia: A Natural History, with Sydney Cannings, Greystone Books, 2004.

The BC Roadside Naturalist, with Sydney Cannings, Greystone Books, 2002.

Life in the Pacific Ocean, with Sydney Cannings and Marja de Jong Westman, Greystone Books, 1999.

The Geology of British Columbia, with Sydney Cannings, Greystone Books, 1999.

Mountains and Northern Forests, with Sydney Cannings, Greystone Books, 1998.

The World of Fresh Water, with Sydney Cannings and Robert Cannings, Greystone Books, 1971.

Birds of Interior BC and the Rockies

Richard Cannings

with

Harry Nehls
Mike Denny
Dave Trochlell

VANCOUVER • VICTORIA • CALGARY

First edition 2009; reprinted 2011, 2013, 2016

Heritage House Publishing Company Ltd.
heritagehouse.ca

LIBRARY AND ARCHIVES CANADA CATALOGUING IN PUBLICATION

Cannings, Richard J. (Richard James)
Birds of interior BC and the Rockies / Richard Cannings; with Harry Nehls, Mike Denny, and Dave Trochlell.
Includes index.
ISBN 978-1-894974-59-2
1. Birds—British Columbia—Identification. 2. Birds—Rocky Mountains, Canadian (B.C. and Alta.)—Identification. I. Nehls, Harry B. II. Denny, Mike III. Trochlell, Dave IV. Title.

QL685.5.B7C37 2009 598.09711 C2009-904039-5

Edited by Jean Wilson
Proofread by Holland Gidney
Cover design by Gina Calle and Frances Hunter
Interior-design template by Gina Calle, modified by One Below
Front-cover photo of Mountain Bluebird by Laure Neish
Back-cover photo of Yellow-headed Blackbird by Gaye Horn

Printed in China

Heritage House acknowledges the financial support for its publishing program from the Government of Canada through the Canada Book Fund (CBF), Canada Council for the Arts, and the Province of British Columbia through the British Columbia Arts Council and the Book Publishing Tax Credit.

Heritage House reconnaissons l'aide financière du gouvernement du Canada par l'entremise du Fonds du livre du Canada et le Conseil des arts du Canada, et de la province de la Colombie-Britannique par le Conseil des arts de la Colombie-Britannique et le Crédit d'impôt pour l'édition de livres.

Canada

The Canada Council for the Arts | Le Conseil des Arts du Canada

BRITISH COLUMBIA ARTS COUNCIL
Supported by the Province of British Columbia

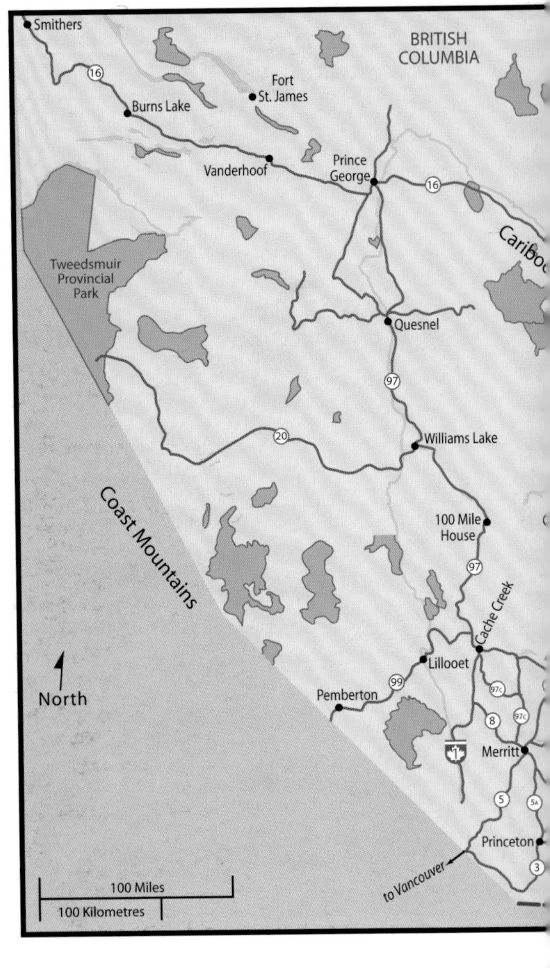

The geographic area covered i

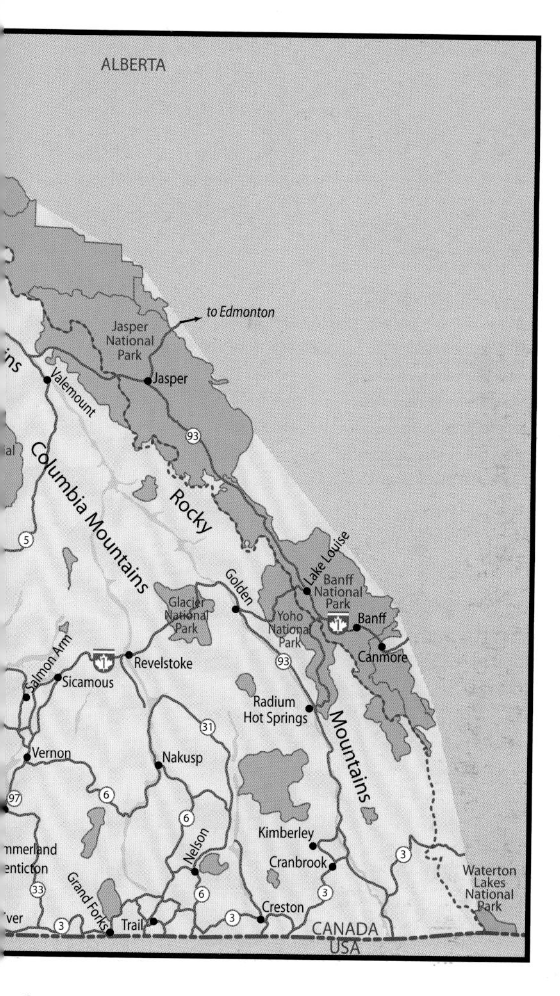

of Interior BC and the Rockies.

Common Local Birds

Here are some of the most common birds in Interior British Columbia and the Rockies. For more information about each bird, go to its Species Account.

Mallard
p. 37

Red-tailed Hawk
p. 117

American Coot
p. 127

American Kestrel
p. 121

California Quail
p. 81

Canada Goose
p. 29

Common Nighthawk
p. 207

American Crow
p. 267

Great Blue Heron
p. 101

Common Raven
p. 269

Killdeer
p. 133

Black-billed Magpie
p. 265

Western Kingbird
p. 251

Northern Flicker
p. 235

Rock Pigeon
p. 175

American Goldfinch
p. 417

Mourning Dove
p. 177

Black-capped Chickadee
p. 285

Mountain Chickadee
p. 285

Western Meadowlark
p. 395

American Robin
p. 319

Tree Swallow
p. 273

Barn Swallow
p. 283

Bohemian Waxwing
p. 331

Cedar Waxwing
p. 331

European Starling
p. 327

White-crowned Sparrow
p. 379

Dark-eyed Junco
p. 383

House Finch
p. 411

Brewer's Blackbird
p. 399

Bullock's Oriole
p. 403

Red-winged Blackbird
p. 393

Introduction

Birdwatching, or birding, has become one of Canada's most popular outdoor activities. It is estimated that one-fifth of all North Americans—50 million people—either watch or feed birds. Birding can be great family entertainment. It is easy to get started, inexpensive, healthy, and allows us to understand and appreciate the natural world. *Birds of Interior BC and the Rockies* is for beginning birdwatchers who wish to identify the regularly occurring birds of the region. This guide will also appeal to experienced birders who wish to learn more about the behaviour, habitats, and seasonal occurrence of local birds.

Given the popularity of birdwatching and the region's beauty, it is little wonder that residents and visitors enjoy seeing and studying the rich variety of local bird life. Over 260 species of birds are permanent residents or regular annual visitors. These are the birds featured in this guide.

Geographical Coverage

Birds of Interior BC and the Rockies covers the Interior of British Columbia from the Canada–US border north to Prince George and the Rocky Mountains of BC and Alberta north to Kakwa Provincial Park. The western boundary of the region is roughly the crest of the Cascade and Coast Mountains, from Manning Provincial Park north to Smithers; the eastern boundary is the eastern edge of the Rockies. The region does not include the foothills of the Rockies. The term "region," as used in this guide, refers to this entire geographical area, as depicted on the map on pages vi–vii.

Conservation

Increased development of the region's urban and rural communities has led to changes in habitat and habitat loss, impacting local bird populations. Grassland and riparian habitats in the valley bottoms have suffered the greatest irrevocable impact, while mature forests have declined in extent throughout the region. The recent mountain pine beetle epidemic has radically altered the forests there. Some bird populations have seen declines of up to 80 percent over the last 20 years. A diverse and thriving bird life is an excellent indicator of a healthy environment. Those who enjoy birds should do all they can to protect birds and their habitats. We urge you to join one of the many conservation organizations that strive to address and improve environmental conditions.

- Local naturalist club (www.bcnature.ca)
- Wild Bird Nature Trust (www.wildbirdtrust.org)
- The Nature Trust of British Columbia (www.naturetrust.bc.ca)
- The Land Conservancy (www.conservancy.bc.ca)
- Nature Conservancy of Canada (www.natureconservancy.ca)

Two other regional conservation organizations are:

- Okanagan Similkameen Conservation Alliance (www.osca.org)
- WildSight (www.wildsight.ca).

Identifying Birds

It can be confusing when you first start trying to identify birds. First, look at the general shape, size, and colour of the bird. Check Common Local Birds (pages ix–xiv) and see if it is there. If not, scan through the Species Account pages for your bird. Read the description—especially the **boldfaced** text—to see how it matches your bird. Compare range, similar species, and habitat. Keep comparing your bird to the book until you have a match.

The different colours of a bird's feathering ("plumage") and bare parts (bill, legs, feet) provide one of the best ways to identify a bird. Most of the plumages and colour patterns for bird species are unique. However, plumages may vary within the same species between the sexes, between adults and younger birds, and by season.

In some species the male and the female have distinctly different plumages. Good examples are the Mallard, House Finch, Red-winged Blackbird, and Rufous Hummingbird. Usually the males have the most brilliant colours, as in these examples, while the females have muted colours so they are not easily detected as they incubate eggs and raise young. Other species such as the Rock Pigeon, Steller's Jay, American Crow, and Song Sparrow show no plumage differences between the sexes.

Most birds seen in Interior British Columbia and the Rockies in spring and summer display what is known as their summer or "breeding" plumage. Birds seen here in winter are usually in their "non-breeding" or winter plumage. Typically, but not always, the breeding plumage is more colourful or highly patterned and the non-breeding plumage is more muted.

Moulting is the process of replacing worn feathers with new, fresh feathers. Most local birds replace some or all of their feathers in a moult in summer or early fall when they change into their non-breeding plumage. Many birds moult again in late winter or spring

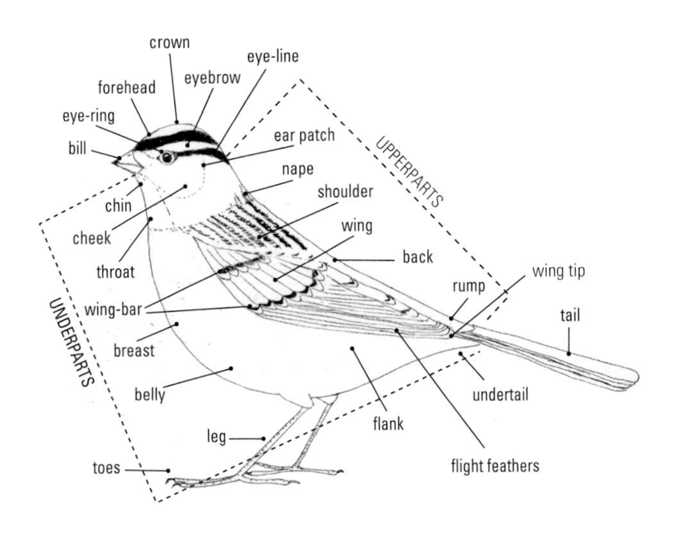

Parts of a Bird. It is helpful to know the names of the different parts of a bird. These sketches of a White-crowned Sparrow and an in-flight Mallard show the terms used to describe bird anatomy in this guide.

when they change into their breeding plumage. These moults occur over a period of several weeks or months.

Some birds have different plumages as they mature. This is particularly true for gulls, which take up to four years and several plumage stages to gain their adult plumage.

The term "juvenile" refers to a newborn bird after it loses its initial downy feathers. Some species hold this plumage for only a

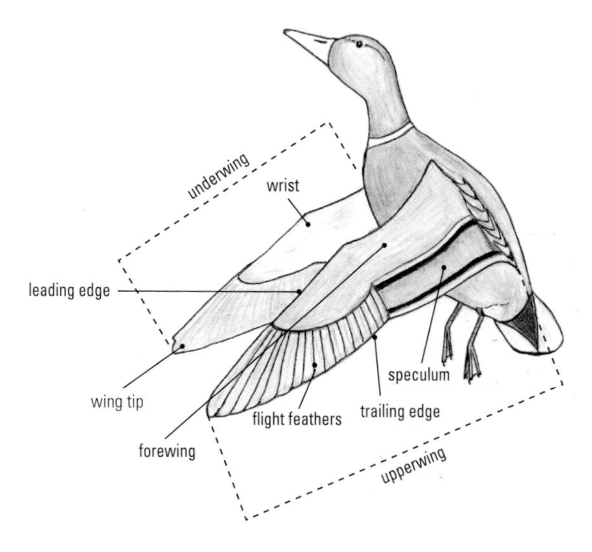

few weeks after fledging while others may hold it into winter. "First-year" refers to the plumage held during the first 12 months of a bird's life. "Immature" refers to all plumages before the bird gains its adult plumage.

Colours and patterning may vary considerably among birds of the same species and plumage stage, especially when they belong to different geographical populations. For instance, the Peregrine Falcons that nest in the Arctic and migrate through the region are distinctly paler than the Peregrines that nest within the region. Differences can be great even within the same local population. The majority of Red-tailed Hawks in the region have light breasts and underwings, yet a certain percentage of birds have dark-brown underparts and dark underwings with lighter-coloured flight feathers. Such consistently different types are called "colour morphs" (or just morphs).

In this book birds are presented in family groupings, as shown in the Quick Guide to Local Birds on the first page. Beginning birders will find that learning the characteristics of the different bird families will make bird identification both easier and quicker. Birds in the same family look similar and often behave in a similar manner. Hummingbirds, for example, are all small, with long, thin bills, have fast wingbeats, and can hover. Once you see a bird with these characteristics, you are well on your way to identifying it as a hummingbird.

Don't expect every bird you see to look exactly like the photographs in this guide. Birds, like people, are individuals. To appreciate how variable birds of the same species can be, study the ones that come regularly to your backyard feeder. Male House Finches, for example, can show a wide range of coloration, from rich, deep red to golden yellow. You may find that, with practice, you can learn to recognize individual birds by the subtle differences in their markings.

Binoculars

Binoculars are a great help in getting good views of birds. Binoculars come in many sizes. Each is labelled with two numbers, e.g., 7 x 35, 8 x 40, 10 x 50. The first number is the magnification. You may think that the larger the magnification, the better the binoculars. However, as magnification increases, clarity may diminish as well as brightness and field of view (the width of the area you can see at a given distance). Another trade-off is that the higher-powered binoculars are usually heavier, hence harder to hold steady or carry for extended periods of time.

The second number is the diameter of the big lens (objective) in millimetres. The larger the diameter, the greater the light-gathering capability of the binoculars and the more colours and details you can see, especially in poor light conditions.

Many discount stores offer binoculars in the $50 to $100 price range, which may be suitable for beginning birders. Higher-quality binoculars are available at nature stores and camera shops and cost from $200 to $1,500. Remember that inexpensive binoculars are easily damaged and provide poorer image quality; the more expensive ones can be knocked around somewhat with no ill effects, are moisture-proof, and offer superior images—you get what you pay for!

The best way to select binoculars is to go to a store that has a good selection and try out several kinds. If you wear glasses, fold, screw, or snap down the eyecups to get your pupil closer to the lens so you get a larger image. Look at a sign at the other end of the store and see which binoculars provide the sharpest image. There should be no distortion in either shape or colour. Which ones feel most comfortable in your hands? Is it easy to change focus? Can you focus on close objects (within 3–4 metres)? Which pair is the most durable and has the largest field of view?

Out in the field, examine what other birders are using and ask for the opportunity to look through their binoculars. Selecting binoculars is a personal thing—what is comfortable for you may not be the same for another birder. So choose ones that have sufficient magnification (7 or 8 power), a wide objective lens (35 millimetres or more), an acceptable field of view (100 metres or more at 1,000 metres), are easy to use, and fit your budget. A good rule of thumb is to buy the best binoculars you can afford.

Also, make sure you get a wide strap (at least 2.5 centimetres). It will help prevent a sore neck by the end of the day. Even better are some of the harnesses that transfer weight to the shoulders rather than the neck. Binoculars also come with dust covers for each of the four lenses.

Finally, take time to adjust the focus of your binoculars to your eyes. Do this by adjusting the central focus knob and the eyepiece focus until images appear sharp through both lenses.

Attracting Birds to Your Yard

Most people get involved in birdwatching by observing the birds that appear in their yards. Perhaps the easiest way to see birds is to put up feeders and watch for birds to appear. When they are perched and eating, birds tend to stay long enough for you to study their field marks at close range and identify them.

Although just hanging out a birdseed feeder will attract some birds, a complete backyard bird program has three important requirements: **food**, **water**, and **shelter**. By paying careful attention to all three of these elements you will not only increase the number and variety of birds that visit your yard, but you will also be contributing to their well-being. Many helpful books and brochures on bird feeding, nest boxes, and gardening for wildlife are available at nature stores and nurseries.

Food

The food that birds eat comes mainly from natural sources. Native and ornamental shrubs, trees, and other plants provide fruits, seeds, flowers, and insects. You will attract more birds to your yard by selecting plants favourable to birds.

You may also provide seeds, suet, and other products to entice birds to your yard. Many seeds are suitable for feeding birds although the best product for this region is black-oil sunflower seed, which has a high fat content. Many grocery and hardware stores sell a birdseed mix that contains some black-oil sunflower seed but often has a lot of millet (the small, round, tan-coloured seed) and filler grains. When you place this seed in a hanging feeder 1.5–1.8 metres off the ground, some of the birds will eat only the sunflower seed and kick the filler and millet to the ground. In elevated feeders, it is much better to use only black-oil sunflower seed or a specialized mix of seeds that is high in nutritional value.

Different birds have different feeding preferences. You may wish to try more than one of the following common feeder types, depending on the species of birds you wish to attract.

- **Fly-through and hopper feeders** are hung or mounted on a pole or deck normally 1.5–1.8 metres above the ground. Stocked with black-oil sunflower seed, they attract Steller's Jay, finches, Red-breasted Nuthatch, and chickadees.
- A **ground feeder or platform feeder** is placed near the ground or up to table height and filled with millet, corn, or a birdseed mix that has some black-oil sunflower seeds but is mostly millet. This feeder will attract quail, pheasants, doves, pigeons, ducks, sparrows, Dark-eyed Junco, Spotted Towhee, and Red-winged Blackbird.
- Cylindrical **tube feeders** are either hung or mounted and can be filled with a nutritional mix of birdseed or just black-oil sunflower seed. They attract the smaller birds such as Red-breasted Nuthatch, Pine Siskin, chickadees, and finches.
- A specialized tube feeder to hold niger thistle seed is called a **thistle or finch feeder** and can attract numbers of small finches such as Pine Siskin and American Goldfinch.
- **Suet**, either acquired at a local meat market or purchased at a nature store in suet cakes, attracts woodpeckers, Red-breasted Nuthatch, chickadees, Bushtit, and a host of other birds seeking its high-energy fat.
- **Hummingbird feeders** attract the three species of hummingbirds that breed in Interior British Columbia and the Rockies. It is easy to make hummingbird nectar: mix one part sugar to three or four parts water, boil, let cool, and then fill your feeders. Do not add any artificial food colouring; the red of the feeder is sufficient to attract hummingbirds.

Experiment with your feeder locations and different birdseed to learn what works best in your yard. Feeders should be placed close to natural shelters such as bushes and trees so the birds can escape from predators. You can feed the birds all year long without worrying that your bird feeding will delay the birds' migration. They will leave when the time is right.

Water

Birds need water for bathing and drinking. You will find that you attract more birds if you offer a reliable source of clean water in your yard. Consider placing a concrete birdbath filled with two or three centimetres of water to meet their needs. Clean and refill it regularly. Be sure the bottom surface is rough so birds can get a good footing. Place the birdbath near shrubs or trees where they can preen after bathing and escape from predators. Try adding a dripper to the birdbath. The sound of dripping water attracts birds.

Shelter and Nest Boxes

Birds need cover so they can seek protection from bad weather and predators. Nearby bushes, shrubs, and trees will help meet their needs as will a loosely stacked brush pile. Neighbourhood cats can be a real problem, especially when they lurk beneath feeders and birdbaths. Careful placement or screening off of feeders and birdbaths, or placing chicken wire strategically in front of favourite cat stalking areas, will help protect birds.

Some of the birds featured in this guide are cavity-nesters and may be enticed to use a birdhouse, which you can either build yourself or purchase at a nature store. It is important to realize that there is no such thing as a generic nest box. Different birds have different needs, and each nest box has to meet the demands of its occupant or it will not be used. The size of the opening and its height above the floor are critical, as is the height of the nest box above the ground. Some nest boxes also serve as wintering roosting boxes for smaller birds. It may take a season or two to attract chickadees, nuthatches, or swallows to your nest boxes. Once they start nesting on your property, you will enjoy watching the behaviour of these nesting birds.

Hygiene

Feeders, the ground below the feeders, and birdbaths need to be cleaned on a regular basis to eliminate the possibility of the spread of avian diseases. Scrub feeders and birdbaths with soap and water. Mix 1 part bleach to 10 parts hot water to sanitize them. Rinse them well then let them dry completely before refilling.

Be sure to inspect nest boxes each fall and give them a good cleaning, but use no insecticides. Discard used nesting materials. Repair any damage so that the boxes are ready and waiting for their new occupants to arrive in the spring.

Observing Birds

Many birdwatchers are quite content just to watch the birds in their yards casually. Some, however, get more involved and begin to look for birds beyond their immediate neighbourhoods. To get the most out of birding in the field, look, listen, and move slowly. Try to keep conversations to a minimum.

To help locate birds, watch for their movement and listen for their calls. Most often we see birds fly to a nearby branch or flit around in a tree. Their movement catches our attention. But an important part of birdwatching is listening and, many times, it is a bird's song or call that draws us to it.

Bird songs are a good way to identify birds. Each bird species has a unique song, and, with practice, you can learn to differentiate the songs. You can purchase digital audio files or CDs that allow you to study bird vocalizations at your leisure. With experience, you will be able to identify birds simply by their songs and calls.

When to Go Birding

Small birds tend to be most active when they are feeding early in the morning (as early as daybreak). Hawks become active in the morning after the rising temperature creates thermals that allow them to soar through the air. Most owls are nocturnal and are most active in the evening or just before dawn.

Birds vary with the season. Some species stay in the region throughout the year while others arrive in the spring and leave in the fall. Other species migrate into the lowlands of the area from the north, the mountains, or the interior of the continent and spend the winter.

Spring is a great time of year. The flowers are blooming, the trees are budding, and the birds, in their bright breeding plumages, are returning from their wintering grounds. The males start singing and the local nesting birds seek mates, breed, and start to raise their families. Hummingbirds feed on flower nectar or at feeders. Wintering birds head north to their breeding grounds.

In summer, the local young birds hatch, and their parents are busy feeding them. As summer progresses, the young learn to fly and fend for themselves. By August, summer visitors are beginning to head south to their wintering grounds.

By late summer, most of the Arctic-breeding shorebirds have passed through on their way south. As fall changes to winter, flocks of waterfowl leave the breeding lakes of the central Interior and appear on the large southern lakes. Resident birds continue to use neighbourhood bird feeders, joined by winter visitors driven down to the lowlands by snowfall in the mountains.

Keeping Records

Keeping a birding journal is an excellent way to get more enjoyment out of your interest. It is simple to keep a list of the birds seen around your yard every day—you'll be surprised how a little bit of focused attention can tune you in to birds' daily and seasonal movements and behaviours. There are several computer programs (e.g., AviSys, BirdBase) that can help you keep track of things, or use the excellent online program at eBird Canada (www.ebird.ca). These programs will keep track of all the birds you report, so you will know your "life list" (all the birds seen in your lifetime), your "yard list" (all the birds seen from your yard), or any other list you are interested in. As lists grow, so does a sense of personal accomplishment. Along with the pleasure of finding new and different birds comes an incentive to learn more about them. Careful record keeping by knowledgeable observers can contribute greatly to scientific understanding of bird life.

A checklist of local birds is provided on pages 425–429.

Bird Habitats in Interior BC and the Rockies

The place where a bird or other living creature is normally found is termed its "habitat." Birds are quite diverse in their habitat requirements. Brown Creepers are seldom seen over open water or loons in trees. To a large extent, the secret to finding and identifying birds is knowing the habitats and developing an understanding of which birds are likely to be seen where. The more types of habitat you explore, the greater the variety of birds you will see.

The region has nine major habitat categories:

Freshwater, Marsh, and Shore
The British Columbia Interior is blessed with many large and small lakes that are an important habitat for many birds. Ducks, geese, and swans are obvious examples, but loons, grebes, Great Blue Herons, Ospreys, and Belted Kingfishers are also never found far from open water. Most of the marshes in the region are small except for the Columbia wetlands in the East Kootenay and the Creston Valley marshes, but the sheer number of marshy ponds in the Cariboo-Chilcotin are a critical habitat for breeding birds, including American Bitterns, Virginia Rails, Soras, Black Terns, Marsh Wrens, and Red-winged and Yellow-headed Blackbirds.

Dry Coniferous Forest
The open forests of ponderosa pines and Douglas-firs at low elevations in the southern Interior valleys are home to a distinctive bird community. Common Poorwills and Flammulated Owls call through the spring and summer nights, a few White-headed Woodpeckers roam the south Okanagan, and Pygmy Nuthatches, Western Bluebirds, and Cassin's Finches are rarely found far from ponderosa pines.

Wet Coniferous Forest

This habitat includes cedar-hemlock forests at low and middle elevations, especially in the Selkirk, Monashee, Cariboo, and western Purcell ranges and the Rocky Mountain Trench from Tête Jaune Cache north to Prince George. These forests are home to Barred Owls, Hammond's Flycatchers, Steller's Jays, Chestnut-backed Chickadees, Winter Wrens, Golden-crowned Kinglets, Swainson's Thrushes, Varied Thrushes, and Pine Siskins.

Broadleaf Riparian Forest

This habitat includes stands of black cottonwood, trembling aspen, and birch, usually lining the riparian zone along many creeks and larger streams throughout the region. The birds that prefer this habitat include Ruffed Grouse, Western Screech- and Barred Owls, Red-naped Sapsuckers, Downy Woodpeckers, Western Wood-Pewees, Eastern Kingbirds, Warbling and Red-eyed Vireos, Black-capped Chickadees, and Veeries.

Dry Grasslands

Dry grasslands and shrub steppes are found at lower elevations in many of the southern valleys of the region. This is one of the most endangered habitats in Canada, and attracts species such as the Sharp-tailed Grouse, Prairie Falcon, Long-billed Curlew, White-throated Swift, Sage Thrasher, Vesper and Brewer's Sparrows, and Western Meadowlark.

Subalpine Forests, Parkland, and Alpine Meadows

High-elevation forests of Engelmann spruce, subalpine fir and lodgepole pine provide habitat for birds with a northern flavour, such as the Spruce Grouse, Boreal Owl, American Three-toed Woodpecker, Boreal Chickadee, and Pine Grosbeak. Higher still, the forest opens up to meadows with alpine wildflowers and scattered stands of trees. Look here for the White-tailed Ptarmigan, Horned Lark, Mountain Bluebird, American Pipit, Fox Sparrow, and Gray-crowned Rosy-Finch.

Shrubby Thickets

Shrubby thickets exist in clearings and around the edges of coniferous and broadleaf woods, transportation and power-line corridors, and overgrown fencerows. Willow Flycatchers, Gray Catbirds, Orange-crowned and MacGillivray's Warblers, Spotted Towhees, and sparrows live in this habitat.

Parks and Gardens

This urban and suburban habitat attracts many of the birds that come to our backyard bird feeders, including hummingbirds, woodpeckers, chickadees, nuthatches, grosbeaks, House Finches, and American Goldfinches. This habitat also hosts Rock Pigeons, American Crows, American Robins, European Starlings, and House Sparrows.

Farmland and Pastures

The open pastures and agricultural fields of the lowlands host Northern Harriers, Ring-necked Pheasants, Mourning Doves, and wintering hawks and blackbirds.

Birding in Interior BC and the Rockies

One of the best ways to see new birds is to join a local naturalist club on a field trip. Participants often visit new areas, learn how to identify new birds, and meet people who share a common interest.

After studying the birds in your yard, visit local parks and greenbelts. A selection of the top birding locations in the British Columbia Interior and Rockies is listed below. For maps and directions to these and other fine regional birding sites, consult the bird-finding guides, websites, and other resources listed on pages 19–21.

- **Okanagan-Boundary-Similkameen:** Okanagan River oxbows and meadows at north end of Osoyoos Lake, Kilpoola Lake Road west of Osoyoos, Chopaka-Nighthawk border crossing, Mount Kobau, Vaseux Lake, White Lake, Kelowna landfill, Vernon Commonage, Swan Lake.
- **Thompson-Nicola-Shuswap:** Kane Valley, Douglas Lake plateau, Beaver Ranch Flats north of Nicola Lake, Tranquille, Lac du Bois, Salmon Arm Bay, Wells Gray Park.
- **Cariboo-Chilcotin:** Scout Island Nature Centre, Williams Lake; Becher's Prairie, Riske Creek; Gang Ranch-Churn Creek area; Alkali Lake.
- **Fraser Basin and Bulkley Valley:** Cottonwood Island, Prince George; Hudson's Bay Mountain, Smithers; Fraser Lake, Nulki Lake.
- **West Kootenay:** Creston Valley, Mount Revelstoke and Glacier National Parks.
- **East Kootenay:** Columbia wetlands between Cranbrook and Golden; Elizabeth Lake, Cranbrook; Kimberley Nature Park; Moberly Marsh, Golden; Skookumchuck Prairie.
- **Rocky Mountains:** The mountain National Parks (Jasper, Banff, Yoho, Kootenay, and Waterton) provide superb access for mountain birding.

Helpful Resources

There are a number of ways to get additional information about birds and their habitats, bird identification, and good places to go birding. Some of the best information is available through books, birding organizations, websites, and local nature stores. Here are some of our favourites:

Regional Publications

The Atlas of Breeding Birds of Alberta: A Second Look, Federation of Alberta Naturalists, 2007.

R. Wayne Campbell, Neil K. Dawe, Ian McTaggart-Cowan, John M. Cooper, Gary W. Kaiser, and Michael C.E. McNall, *Birds of British Columbia* (4 vols.), Royal British Columbia Museum, Canadian Wildlife Service and UBC Press, 1990, 1997, 2001.

Richard and Sydney Cannings, *British Columbia: A Natural History*, Greystone Books, 1996.

Richard and Sydney Cannings, *The BC Roadside Naturalist*, Greystone Books, 2002.

Robert, Richard and Sydney Cannings, *The Birds of the Okanagan Valley, British Columbia*, Royal British Columbia Museum,1987.

Ben Gadd, *Handbook of the Canadian Rockies*, Corax Press, 1995.

Identification Guides

Field Guide to the Birds of North America (5th ed.), National Geographic Society, 2006.

Kenn Kaufman, *Birds of North America*, Houghton Mifflin, 2000.

Roger Tory Peterson, *A Field Guide to Western Birds* (3rd ed.), Houghton Mifflin, 1990.

David Allen Sibley, *The Sibley Field Guide to Birds of Western North America*, Alfred A. Knopf, 2003.

Other Regional Birding Resources

There are 18 local naturalist clubs in the central and southern Interior of British Columbia and several more in western Alberta. They provide an excellent means to learn more about birds. Most clubs have a newsletter, meetings, and local field trips to search for birds. Many have websites with information about good places to go birding.

For details on the British Columbia clubs:
www.bcnature.ca

The national parks (Jasper, Banff, Kootenay, Yoho, Glacier, Mount Revelstoke, and Waterton) all have information on their websites. Also, the national parks have interpretive centres where staff can help answer questions about birds:
www.pc.gc.ca/progs/np-pn/recherche-search_e.asp?p=1

There are a few other sites in the region with similar offerings:

- Allan Brooks Nature Centre in Vernon
  www.abnc.ca
- Bow Valley Naturalists in the Banff area
  www.bowvalleynaturalists.org
- Creston Valley Wildlife Centre
  www.crestonwildlife.ca
- Osoyoos Desert Centre
  www.desert.org
- Scout Island Nature Centre in Williams Lake
  www.williamslake.ca/index.asp?p=40

The South Okanagan Naturalists' Club has an online Okanagan bird checklist and links to other regional information:
members.tripod.com/~sonc/

The British Columbia Field Ornithologists (BCFO)—open to anyone interested in birds—offers field trips, a newsletter and journal, and an annual conference. Visit the BCFO website for information on membership and upcoming activities:

www.bcfo.ca

Birding in British Columbia is a good webpage that offers a great deal of information on local birding as well as links to other sites:

www.birding.bc.ca

There are numerous e-mail lists on birds and birding; three that are appropriate for the region—albertabirds, bcintbird, and wkbirds—can be joined online at:

groups.yahoo.com

Species Accounts

The following pages present accounts and photographs of the most familiar bird species of the British Columbia Interior and Rockies. Information on each species is presented in a standardized format: see the sample page (opposite) for an explanation. Species are grouped by families, colour-coded, and thumb-indexed. The Quick Guide on the first page inside the front cover of this book will help you locate the birds.

The following terms are used to describe the relative abundance of each species and the likelihood of finding it in a particular season:

- **Common:** Found in moderate to large numbers, and easily found in appropriate habitat at the right time of year.
- **Fairly Common:** Found in small to moderate numbers, and usually easy to find in appropriate habitat at the right time of year.
- **Uncommon:** Found in small numbers, and usually—but not always—found with some effort in appropriate habitat at the right time of year.
- **Rare:** Occurs annually in very small numbers. Not to be expected on any given day, but may be found with extended effort over the course of the appropriate season(s).

Birds shown in the photographs in the Species Accounts are adults unless the captions indicate otherwise.

COMMON NAME
Scientific name

DESCRIPTION: Length (and wingspan for larger species), followed by a description that includes differences in plumages between sexes and ages. Key field marks—unique markings visible in the field that help distinguish one species from another—are shown in **boldfaced** type.

SIMILAR SPECIES: Identifies similar-appearing species and describes how to tell them apart.

VOICE: Describes the main song and calls of the species.

WHERE TO FIND: Describes the general locations and habitats where this bird may be found in the region, often with suggestions of good places to search for the species. Identifies the times of year that the species is present and its relative abundance (see facing page for definitions of abundance terms).

BEHAVIOUR: Highlights behavioural characteristics of the species, including feeding behaviour, distinctive movements and displays, flight style, and breeding behaviour.

DID YOU KNOW? Provides other interesting facts about the species.

DATE AND LOCATION SEEN: A place for you to record the date and location of your first sighting of this species.

Greater White-fronted Goose

Anser albifrons

DESCRIPTION: 71 cm, wingspan 135 cm. **Grey-brown goose** with a **pinkish bill** and bright **orange legs**. The **rear underparts are contrastingly white**, and there is a **white band across the base of the tail**; has narrow white tail tip. ADULT: Has **white feathering at the base of the bill**, **irregular black blotches or speckles across the belly**. JUVENILE: Lacks white on the face and black belly speckles.

SIMILAR SPECIES: Similar-looking domestic geese lack black belly speckles. Canada Goose (p. 29) has a black neck, bill, legs, and broad white chin strap.

VOICE: Common flight call is high, yelping *kah-la-luck*.

WHERE TO FIND: Fairly common spring (March–April) and fall (September–November) migrant in Creston Valley; rarely seen elsewhere or at other times of the year.

BEHAVIOUR: Migrating flocks stage in farm fields along the flyway. Feeds by gleaning grain from fields, grazing grasses, and foraging in shallow water.

DID YOU KNOW? These beautiful geese are called "speckle-bellies" by hunters.

DATE AND LOCATION SEEN: ______________________

____

____

DESCRIPTION: 71 cm, wingspan 135 cm. **Medium-large white goose with black wing tips**. **Pink bill** shows black **grinning patch** along the sides where the mandibles meet. Juvenile is washed in grey on neck, back, and wings; bill is dull pinkish-grey. Rare "Blue" plumage morph is variably slate grey on back, breast, and neck.

SIMILAR SPECIES: Ross's Goose (rare) is very similar but much smaller (Mallard-sized), lacks grinning patch on bill; larger swans and white domestic geese do not have black wing tips.

VOICE: Call is raucous, fairly high yelping *wowk* or *wow*.

WHERE TO FIND: Uncommon migrant (March–April and October–November) through the Interior; most migrate from the Arctic to southern wintering grounds along the coast or east of the Rockies. Usually seen in small numbers with other geese.

BEHAVIOUR: Grazes on grasses, grain, and marsh vegetation; forages in shallow water as well as on land.

DID YOU KNOW? Boosted by plentiful winter food in agricultural areas, many populations of Snow Geese have now become so large that they are heavily impacting their fragile Arctic nesting areas.

DATE AND LOCATION SEEN: ______________________

____

____

Cackling Goose
Canada Goose

Branta canadensis / Branta hutchinsii

DESCRIPTION: 109 cm/56 cm, wingspan 152 cm/109 cm. CANADA: Large brown goose with a pale breast, **black neck**, **white chin strap**, and flat crown. Undertail and band across rump are white. Bill and legs are black. CACKLING: Smaller (Mallard-sized) version of Canada, usually with darker underparts. Has **small**, **stubby bill**, **rounded crown**, and higher, squeakier calls.

SIMILAR SPECIES: Greater White-fronted Goose (p. 25) lacks white chin strap.

VOICE: CANADA: Loud, resonant *ha-ronk*. CACKLING: High-pitched, squeaking *ur-lik*.

WHERE TO FIND: CANADA: Common migrants (October–May) and residents of valleys. Winter mainly in low-elevation southern valleys where food and open water are available. Summer resident around plateau lakes. CACKLING: Uncommon to rare winter residents (October–May) that join Canada Goose flocks.

BEHAVIOUR: Both forage for plants, grains, and invertebrates in wetlands, reservoirs, farmland, and parks. Canada Geese feed and nest in many types of open habitats that provide abundant food resources, water, and sufficient space. Often nest high off the ground on Osprey nest platforms or on cliff ledges above water. Aggressive and territorial in breeding season, Canada Geese form large post-breeding flocks that are joined by Cackling Geese in late fall.

DID YOU KNOW? At least 11 subspecies of Canada Geese were formerly recognized in North America, but in 2004 the four smallest subspecies were elevated to full species status now known as Cackling Geese.

DATE AND LOCATION SEEN: ______________________

____

____

Tundra Swan

Trumpeter Swan

DESCRIPTION: 132 cm/152 cm, wingspan 168 cm/203 cm. **Large**, **white**, **long-necked** waterfowl with black bills. TUNDRA: Crown is rounded, bill profile slightly concave; **forehead feathers form rounded border with bill between eyes**; eyes more distinct from black at bill base; **yellow patch often** (but not always) **shows in front of eye**. Immature is grey, becoming white during spring migration. TRUMPETER: Larger than Tundra. **Crown and bill profile relatively flat; forehead feathers extend to a point between the eyes**; eyes contained within the black area at bill base. Immature retains grey plumage through spring migration.

SIMILAR SPECIES: Introduced Mute Swan (not shown) has distinctive orange bill with black knob at base.

VOICE: TUNDRA: Clear, barking *klooo* or *kwooo*. TRUMPETER: Lower-pitched, like a trombone or low Canada Goose call.

WHERE TO FIND: TUNDRA: Common to uncommon migrant (October–November, February–April). Common to uncommon winter resident along Thompson River and in Okanagan Valley. TRUMPETER: Common to uncommon migrant and local winter resident (October–February). Winter flocks on Stuart River near Fort St. James, Crooked River north of Prince George, Nautley River at Fort Fraser, South Thompson River, and on Okanagan Valley lakes.

BEHAVIOUR: Both typically forage on aquatic plants, seeds, and waste grains. Gregarious, often form flocks of both species.

DID YOU KNOW? Trumpeter Swans nearly extinct by early 20th century, but populations now healthy and generally increasing.

DATE AND LOCATION SEEN: ______________________

____

____

Male
Female

DESCRIPTION: 47 cm, wingspan 76 cm. A distinctive duck with **drooping crest**; appears long-tailed in flight. BREEDING MALE: **Colourful** green, black, and white head pattern; **red bill base and eye-ring**; deep reddish breast bordered behind by vertical black and white bars; glossy black upperparts, tan-yellow sides, and iridescent blue wing patch. NON-BREEDING MALE: (summer, fall) much duller but retains basic pattern. FEMALE: Conspicuous **white patch surrounds eye**, pointed in rear. Grey above, grey-spotted with white below.

SIMILAR SPECIES: Female Hooded Merganser (p. 61) lacks white around eye, streaking on body; has white, not green, in speculum.

VOICE: Calls include various high whistles, squeaks. Female's call is a penetrating *ooEEK* squeal.

WHERE TO FIND: Locally fairly common summer resident (April–September) in wooded lakes, ponds, and river backwaters. Rare and very local in winter on ice-free ponds and lakes.

BEHAVIOUR: Often perches in trees over water, usually in secluded forested wetlands. Feeds on invertebrates, seeds, and fruits in shallow water; does not dive. Nests in natural tree cavities.

DID YOU KNOW? Although Wood Ducks prefer scarce natural tree cavities for nesting, they will readily use nest boxes.

DATE AND LOCATION SEEN: ______________________________

____

____

Eurasian Wigeon
American Wigeon
Male
American Wigeon
Female

DESCRIPTION: 46 cm, wingspan 81 cm. Medium-sized dabbling ducks with short, black-tipped, bluish-grey bills, white forewing patches, and relatively long, pointed tails. Males of both species have white flank patches and **black undertails**. AMERICAN: Male has **greyish head** with **bright green patch behind eye** and **white or buffy forehead**; has **pinkish-brown back and flanks**. Female has **greyish-brown head**, brown breast and flanks, white belly. EURASIAN: Male has **dark rufous head with yellowish forehead**, **grey back and flanks**. Female has **cinnamon-brown head**.

SIMILAR SPECIES: Female Cinnamon Teal (p. 39) has darker, longer bill. Gadwall (p. 37) has white wing patch, longer yellowish bill.

VOICE: AMERICAN: Whistle is *wi-WE-whew*. EURASIAN: Single descending whistle is *wEEEEEEr*.

WHERE TO FIND: AMERICAN: Common breeder and abundant migrant throughout region; locally common winter resident in southern valleys. EURASIAN: Rare winter resident and migrant that accompanies American Wigeon flocks.

BEHAVIOUR: Both eat mostly plant material, often grazing on lawns or fields. Regularly feed on grass in residential parks and golf courses. Also forage in ponds and marshes by skimming surface, rarely dipping. Form large post-breeding season flocks.

DID YOU KNOW? American Wigeons are also known as Baldpates.

DATE AND LOCATION SEEN: ______________________

____

____

Mallard
Male

Mallard
Female

Gadwall
Female (Top) and Male (Bottom)

Anas platyrhynchos / Anas strepera

DESCRIPTION: 58 cm/51 cm, wingspan 89 cm/84 cm. MALLARD: Large, heavy-bodied, with blue speculum bordered in front and back by white; white underwings, orange legs. Male has **green head**, **white neck ring**, **reddish breast**, pale grey body, curled black feathers at base of tail; yellow bill. In late summer male is like female but retains all-yellow bill. Female is mottled brown, with dark line through eye, orange and dusky bill. GADWALL: Medium-sized, plain duck with squarish head, orange legs, white belly, **square white patch on speculum of wing**. Male is **variegated grey** with paler grey head, **black rear end**; dark grey bill. Female is mottled brown and white; **orange sides to bill**; white wing patch visible at rest.

SIMILAR SPECIES: Female Northern Shoveler (p. 39) has blue forewing and longer, wider bill. Female American Wigeon (p. 35) has rich, orangish-brown unmottled breast and grey bill.

VOICE: MALLARD: Female gives familiar loud quack, male's calls are much quieter. GADWALL: Female has a higher-pitched, more nasal quack.

WHERE TO FIND: MALLARD: Common and widespread throughout the year, in winter concentrated at good feeding sites with open water. GADWALL: Fairly common migrant and breeder on marshy lakes and ponds throughout region, rare at northern edge; uncommon and local in winter in southern valleys.

BEHAVIOUR: Both species forage for vegetation in shallow water by "tipping up;" also graze on land.

DID YOU KNOW? Nearly all domestic ducks are derived from Mallards.

DATE AND LOCATION SEEN: ______________________

____

____

Blue-winged Teal
Male
Blue-winged Teal
Female
Cinnamon Teal
Male
Cinnamon Teal
Female

Anas discors / Anas cyanoptera

DESCRIPTION: 41 cm, wingspan 58 cm. Small dabbling ducks with long, wide dark bill, **pale blue forewing patch** and green speculum (visible in flight), and orange-yellow legs. BLUE-WINGED: Male has spotted brown body with a **slate-grey head and bold white face crescent and flank patch**, and black undertail. Female is mottled brown with diffuse, pale facial area behind bill. CINNAMON: Male is **deep cinnamon red nearly throughout**; has red eyes, black undertail. Female is mottled brown with a plain brown head.

SIMILAR SPECIES: Smaller female Green-winged Teal (p. 45) lacks blue forewing. Northern Shoveler (p. 41) is similar, but has oversized, spatulate bill.

VOICE: Females quack, males give low chatter.

WHERE TO FIND: CINNAMON: Common migrants and summer breeders (April–mid-October), uncommon at northern edge of region. BLUE-WINGED: Fairly common migrants and summer breeders, uncommon at northern edge. Both are absent in winter.

BEHAVIOUR: Both species forage in small, shallow wetlands with dense aquatic plants, and nest in low, grassy vegetation near water.

DID YOU KNOW? Blue-winged and Cinnamon Teals are closely related and occasionally interbreed.

DATE AND LOCATION SEEN: ______________________

____

____

Male

Female

DESCRIPTION: 48 cm, wingspan 76 cm. Medium-sized dabbler with **large, spatulate bill**. Large bill gives front-heavy appearance in flight. MALE: Has **green head** with yellow eyes, **white breast**, and **cinnamon sides**. In flight shows light blue-grey forewing with broad white rear border. FEMALE: Mottled brown with broad buffy-white edges to side and flank feathers; grey forewing with narrow white rear border. Female's large, spoon-shaped bill has distinctive orange sides.

SIMILAR SPECIES: Many other female ducks look similar, but none has large, expanded bill.

VOICE: Females quack, males give soft *thup-tup*.

WHERE TO FIND: Common migrant (April–May, August–October), fairly common summer resident, uncommon and local winter resident in southern valleys.

BEHAVIOUR: Flocks feed in shallow water by tipping up or sifting through water and mud with outsized bills used in sweeping motions. Groups often swim in tight, circling masses with their heads underwater, capturing food stirred up from below. Flocks fly in bunches or loose lines.

DID YOU KNOW? Northern Shovelers have fringes along the sides of the bill that help them filter food items from water and mud.

DATE AND LOCATION SEEN: ______________________

____

____

Male
Female

DESCRIPTION: 53 cm, wingspan 84 cm. Slender, **long-necked dabbling duck** with a **grey bill** and long, pointed tail. MALE: **Brown head**, white breast, **white stripes extending up the sides of the neck**. Grey body with elongated black and white feathers on sides of back; black undertail, **long pointed central tail feathers**. Coppery-green speculum, bordered in front by buff, behind by white. FEMALE: Plain pale brown head and neck, mottled grey-brown body; **central tail feathers pointed**. In flight shows white trailing edge to inner wing; bill is plain grey.

SIMILAR SPECIES: Other dabbling ducks have shorter, stockier necks and lack the pointed tail. Female Redhead (p. 47) is stockier, more solidly grey-brown on the body, and has pale grey flight feathers.

VOICE: Female gives hoarse quacks. Male gives a thin, wheezy whistle and a musical *droop* call, often doubled.

WHERE TO FIND: Common migrant (March–April, September–November), uncommon summer resident throughout region, rare in winter in southern valleys.

BEHAVIOUR: Feeds by tipping up, with long tail pointed skyward and head and neck underwater. Flies in lines or Vs, appearing slim and long-necked.

DID YOU KNOW? Northern Pintails are one of the earliest nesting ducks, often laying eggs in northern areas as soon as the ice has melted on nesting ponds.

DATE AND LOCATION SEEN: ______________________

____

____

Male
Female

DESCRIPTION: 36 cm, wingspan 58 cm. Smallest dabbling duck. All show bright **green speculum** with buffy-white border in front. Bill is small and dark. MALE: **Bright green ear patch** borders **chestnut crown and face**; body is grey with **white vertical stripe behind breast**; undertail is pale yellow and black. FEMALE: Mottled brown; dark line through eye bordered indistinctly by buffy-brown lines; buffy patch is on sides of undertail.

SIMILAR SPECIES: Female Cinnamon (p. 39) and Blue-winged Teals (p. 39) have larger bills and blue-grey forewing patch, and lack buff or whitish patch below tail.

VOICE: Male's call is high *dreep*. Female's call is short, rough *quack*.

WHERE TO FIND: Common migrant (March–May, August–October), uncommon summer resident in marshes throughout region; uncommon to fairly common winter resident in southern valleys.

BEHAVIOUR: Forages by dabbling at surface of shallow water, also feeds shorebird-style on mud flats. Springs vertically from the water when disturbed. Mostly migratory, though many remain farther north during the winter than other species of teal.

DID YOU KNOW? Male Eurasian Green-winged Teals (Common Teal) have a white horizontal stripe above the wing instead of the vertical breast stripe. Rarely appear in winter flocks with American Green-winged Teal.

DATE AND LOCATION SEEN: ______________________

____

____

Canvasback
Male
Canvasback
Female
Redhead
Male
Redhead
Female

CANVASBACK / REDHEAD

Aythya valisineria / Aythya americana

DESCRIPTION: 53 cm/48 cm, wingspan 74 cm. CANVASBACK: Male has **nearly whitish body**, **deep chestnut head**, red eyes, **long**, **sloping forehead**, **and long**, **black bill**. Female is pale grey with light brown head and chest, pale grey wings. REDHEAD: Male is **medium grey** with **bright rufous-red head**, rounded forehead, and shorter **blue-grey bill with black tip** preceded by a white line. Female is plain grey-brown; **pale grey flight feathers contrast with darker forewing**.

SIMILAR SPECIES: Female Greater and Lesser Scaup (p. 51), Ring-necked Duck (p. 49) similar to female Redhead, but have distinct white patches at the base of their bills.

VOICE: Both species generally quiet, but male Redheads in wintering flocks give a soft, meowing *weeew* call while courting.

WHERE TO FIND: CANVASBACK: Fairly common but local migrant and wintering species (September–April) in southern valleys. Uncommon to locally common summer resident on marshy plateau lakes. REDHEAD: Common migrant and summer resident (March–October); uncommon at northern edges of region. Locally abundant in winter in Okanagan Valley.

BEHAVIOUR: Both species dive underwater in marshes, ponds, and lakes for aquatic plants and invertebrates. They form large, mixed flocks with other wintering diving ducks.

DID YOU KNOW? Female Redheads sometimes lay their eggs in the nests of other Redheads, or in the nests of other duck species.

DATE AND LOCATION SEEN: ______________________

____

____

Male
Female

DESCRIPTION: 43 cm, wingspan 64 cm. Has grey bill with **white rings at base and near tip**, bill tip is black; **head is peaked at rear of crown**. In flight, grey flight feathers contrast with darker forewing. MALE: Black with **white crescent behind black breast**, has pale grey sides, head glossed purple, chestnut neck ring difficult to see. FEMALE: Slate grey above, brown below; has white eye-ring, and diffuse, white feathering at base of bill that contrasts with grey face.

SIMILAR SPECIES: Differs from Scaups (p. 51) in having white rings on bill, much more peaked crown, and lacking white wing stripes. Male Scaups have grey (not black) back, whitish (not grey) sides; female Scaups have distinct white patch at bill base and lack an eye-ring.

VOICE: Generally silent.

WHERE TO FIND: Common migrant (October–April), common to uncommon breeder and summer resident; locally common winter resident in southern valleys.

BEHAVIOUR: Favours shallower water and more heavily vegetated sites where it forages for aquatic plants and invertebrates. Sometimes flocks with Scaups and other diving ducks. Usually forms small flocks.

DID YOU KNOW? Ring-necked Duck males have bright yellow eyes, whereas the eyes of females are brown.

DATE AND LOCATION SEEN: ______________________

____

____

Female
Greater Scaup
Male

Female
Lesser Scaup
Male

Greater Scaup / Lesser Scaup

Aythya marila / Aythya affinis

DESCRIPTION: 46 cm/43 cm, wingspan 71 cm/66 cm. Short-necked diving ducks with bluish-grey bills, and **white wing stripes** visible in flight. MALES: **Blackish on both ends**, **whitish in middle**, head darkly iridescent. FEMALES: Brownish with **white facial patch at bill base**. GREATER: **Head** is **round**, neck thicker, bill wider, male's head glosses greenish. LESSER: **Peaked crown**, neck thinner, bill smaller, **wing stripe extends only halfway to wing tip**, male's head glosses purple.

SIMILAR SPECIES: Ring-necked Duck (p. 49) head is more peaked, has ring near bill tip; male has black back, vertical white mark on side.

VOICE: Grating sounds, deep whistles.

WHERE TO FIND: GREATER: Common migrant (April–May, September–November) on larger lakes throughout region and locally common winter resident on large, ice-free southern lakes. LESSER: Common migrant on ponds and smaller lakes throughout region, uncommon to rare winter resident on ice-free rivers and lakes (usually smaller lakes) in southern valleys. Common to uncommon breeding duck on marshy lakes throughout region, particularly on Cariboo-Chilcotin Plateau.

BEHAVIOUR: Both dive for molluscs, other aquatic animals, plants. Highly gregarious, gathering in tight flocks, often including both scaup species, other ducks. LESSER: Nests in shallow wetlands, with nest constructed on nearby dry uplands. In winter, most often seen on larger open rivers and smaller lakes, including sewage ponds.

DID YOU KNOW? Hunters refer to both scaups as "bluebills."

DATE AND LOCATION SEEN: ______________________

Harlequin Duck
Male

Harlequin Duck
Female

Long-tailed Duck
Male

Long-tailed Duck
Female

Harlequin Duck / Long-tailed Duck

Histrionicus histrionicus / Clangula hyemalis

DESCRIPTION: 42 cm, wingspan 66 cm/71 cm. Striking ducks that winter along seacoasts. HARLEQUIN: Male **bluish-grey** except for **chestnut sides** and **white stripes and spots** on breast, face, and wings. Female and young dark brown with **two or three smudgy spots on face**. LONG-TAILED: Spring male is **largely black** with reddish-brown scapulars, white cheek, **very long black tail**; winter male is **largely white with dark face patches**, black and white back, black lower breast, long black tail. Female has short tail. Spring female is mostly brown with **conspicuous white spectacle**, similar in winter but face is white with **dark smudge on lower cheek**.

SIMILAR SPECIES: Female Scoters (p. 55) have multiple white spots on face, but are much larger than Harlequins, with larger bills.

VOICE: HARLEQUIN: female has quacking calls, males a squeaky whistle. LONG-TAILED: females give soft quacks, call of males an unmistakeable *oh OW KOWeLEP*.

WHERE TO FIND: HARLEQUIN: Uncommon summer resident (April–October) throughout region, on fast-moving streams; migrants often rest on lakes. Rare in winter on southern rivers. LONG-TAILED: Uncommon migrant (May, October–November) on lakes in north, rare migrant and winter resident on southern lakes.

BEHAVIOUR: HARLEQUIN: Forages for aquatic insect larvae in creeks and rivers, nest along river banks. LONG-TAILED: Dives for crustaceans and molluscs; nests around tundra ponds and lakes.

DID YOU KNOW? The call of the Long-tailed Duck gave rise to both its former English name—Oldsquaw (ironically from the talkative nature of the males)—and French name—*kakawi*.

DATE AND LOCATION SEEN: ______________________

____

____

White-winged Scoter
Male
White-winged Scoter
Female
Surf Scoter
Male
Surf Scoter
Female

White-winged Scoter / Surf Scoter

Melanitta fusca / Melanitta perspicillata

DESCRIPTION: 53 cm/51 cm, wingspan 88 cm/76 cm. **Large-billed, dark** ducks that winter on seacoasts. WHITE-WINGED: male all black except for **white secondaries** and small **white eye patch**; bill orange with small black knob at base. Female **dark brown with heavy black bill**, two pale smudges on face and **white secondaries**. SURF: Wings all dark. Male unmistakeable; **all black except for huge multicoloured bill**, white forehead, and **white nape patch**. Female dark brown with white face smudges.

SIMILAR SPECIES: No other ducks have such heavy bills.

VOICE: Generally silent in region; females give croaking quacks, males give clear whistles.

WHERE TO FIND: WHITE-WINGED: Common to rare migrant (late April–early June, September–November) throughout region (more common in north), uncommon summer resident on marshy lakes on the Cariboo-Chilcotin and Douglas Lake plateaus. SURF: Common to rare migrant (April–May, October–November) seen resting on lakes throughout region (more common in north).

BEHAVIOUR: Both dive for crustaceans and molluscs; nest in heavy shrubs near lakes.

DID YOU KNOW? The Surf Scoter is endemic to North America, whereas White-winged and Black Scoters are also found in Eurasia.

DATE AND LOCATION SEEN: ______________________

____

____

Male

Female

DESCRIPTION: 33 cm, wingspan 53 cm. Region's **smallest duck**, with a small, grey bill. MALE: White below and mostly black above. Has a large **white area on the back of its head** and a large white wing patch. FEMALE: Dark grey all over with an **oval white cheek patch** and a small white speculum.

SIMILAR SPECIES: Larger Common Goldeneye (p. 59) male has white patch at base of bill; female is grey-bodied and lacks white cheek patch.

VOICE: Generally silent.

WHERE TO FIND: Common migrant and winter resident (November–May) in southern valleys; common summer resident in Cariboo, Chilcotin, and Fraser plateaus, uncommon elsewhere.

BEHAVIOUR: Dives for aquatic invertebrates and small fish in small, loose flocks. Nests in tree cavities or duck nesting boxes beside high-elevation forested lakes. Widespread in winter on lowland lakes and sewage ponds.

DID YOU KNOW? Buffleheads rarely leave the water to walk on the ground.

DATE AND LOCATION SEEN: ______________________

____

____

Common Goldeneye
Male

Common Goldeneye
Female

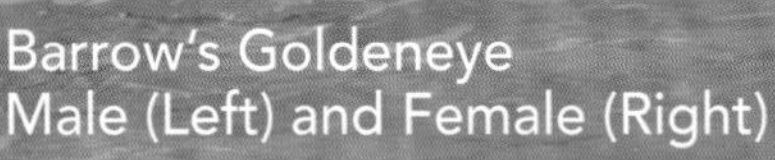

Barrow's Goldeneye
Male (Left) and Female (Right)

Common Goldeneye / Barrow's Goldeneye

Bucephala clangula / Bucephala islandica

DESCRIPTION: 46 cm, wingspan 69 cm. Chunky, medium-sized diving ducks with **white patches at the base of the wings** and yellow eyes. Males are mostly white with black and white upperparts; have dark, iridescent, puffy heads with white face patches. Females are greyish with brown heads. COMMON: **Greenish-black head** is **peaked in middle of crown**; has **round white face patch**; has less black on back. Female has similarly shaped head and yellow-tipped bill much of the year. BARROW'S: **Purplish-black head** is **peaked at forehead**; has **crescent-shaped white face patch**. Female has a similarly shaped head and entirely orange bill much of the year.

SIMILAR SPECIES: Smaller male Bufflehead (p. 57) has large white patch on back of its head; female Buffleheads have white ear patch.

VOICE: Females of both species give low, grating *arr arr* calls.

WHERE TO FIND: COMMON: Common migrant throughout region (October–November, April–May); common winter resident on southern lakes and rivers, uncommon in north; uncommon summer resident on northern plateaus and in Rocky Mountain Trench; rare in summer elsewhere. BARROW'S: Common migrant and local winter resident (October–April), common breeding bird on mountain and plateau lakes throughout region. Very rare in winter in north; most wintering birds are on southern rivers.

BEHAVIOUR: Both eat aquatic invertebrates. Nest in tree cavities near lakes and ponds.

DID YOU KNOW? Most of the world's Barrow's Goldeneyes nest in British Columbia.

DATE AND LOCATION SEEN: ______________________

____

____

Male

Female

DESCRIPTION: 46 cm. Small, thin-billed, long-tailed diving duck. MALE: **Puffy white crest is outlined in black**; when folded back, white of crest is reduced to a long, thick stripe. Black above, tawny on sides, with **two vertical black bars on sides of white breast**. FEMALE: Dusky above, grey-brown on breast and sides; belly is white; **puffy light tawny-brown crest**; bill has much yellow on sides. Immature male like female but with black bill and a hint of adult's head pattern.

SIMILAR SPECIES: Bufflehead (p. 57) has bright white sides with a stubby grey bill. Other mergansers are much larger with red bills.

VOICE: Generally silent, males emit frog-like croaks during courtship.

WHERE TO FIND: Fairly common and widespread migrant, fairly common to rare summer resident. Uncommon and local winter resident (October–March) in open water areas, mostly in southern valleys.

BEHAVIOUR: Dives for small fish and aquatic invertebrates. Nests in tree cavities and nest boxes along woodland streams, swamps, and ponds. Secretive during the nesting season; they move to open-water areas in winter where they sometimes form small flocks.

DID YOU KNOW? They sometimes lay their eggs in the nest cavities of other Hooded Mergansers or even those of other cavity-nesting ducks.

DATE AND LOCATION SEEN: ______________________

____

____

Common Merganser
Male
Common Merganser
Female
Red-breasted Merganser
Male
Red-breasted Merganser
Female

DESCRIPTION: 64 cm/58 cm, wingspan 88 cm/76 cm. Diving ducks with long, slender bills that have saw-like edges. COMMON: **Bill deep-based** and **bright red**. Adult male has **green head** with short, smooth crest; **body mostly white** with black down centre of back. Female and young male have **deep rusty head and neck sharply separated from white chin and chest**; grey breast and flanks. RED-BREASTED: **Bill reddish-orange**. Adult male has **dark green head with shaggy**, **thin crest**, white neck ring, mottled reddish-brown breast bordered behind by black and white patch; mostly blackish above, grey and white below with much white in the wing. Female and young male show **tawny-brown head with thin**, **shaggy crest**, grey body.

SIMILAR SPECIES: Only likely to be confused with each other.

VOICE: Both species are usually silent, but male Common makes low croaking calls.

WHERE TO FIND: COMMON: Common migrant on lakes throughout region, and winter resident on lakes and large rivers in southern valleys, more uncommon on northern rivers. Uncommon to common summer resident on large rivers and lakes. RED-BREASTED: Uncommon to rare migrant and winter resident (September–May), mainly on large ice-free rivers and lakes.

BEHAVIOUR: Both species dive for fish, which they catch and hold with their "saw-toothed" bills. Sometimes flocks move together, herding fish. Nest in tree cavities and holes in cliffs along shorelines.

DID YOU KNOW? Merganser "teeth" are simply projections on the horny covering of the bill, and not actually teeth.

DATE AND LOCATION SEEN: ______________________

____

____

Male
Female

DESCRIPTION: 38 cm. Small duck with a long, **stiff tail, often pointed upward**. MALE: Blackish crown, **large white cheek patch**. Mainly grey-brown (darker above), except the **body is entirely deep chestnut-coloured** and **bill is sky blue** when breeding. FEMALE: Resembles non-breeding male, but with **dark line across whitish cheek**.

SIMILAR SPECIES: Female Bufflehead (p. 57) is greyer with smaller white cheek patch and shorter tail.

VOICE: Male displays with an accelerating series of low, popping notes ending in a low croak: *fup fup fup fupfuf-fuf-fuf-frrrrp.*

WHERE TO FIND: Common summer resident and migrant (April–October) on marshy lakes and ponds, uncommon at northern end of region. Rare and local in winter on ice-free southern lakes.

BEHAVIOUR: Dives for aquatic plants, as well as small fish and invertebrates. More likely to dive rather than fly when approached. Displaying males point tails straight upward and bob their heads in time with vocalizations.

DID YOU KNOW? Ruddy Ducks lay the largest eggs of any waterfowl proportionate to their size; the young are very precocious and can dive to catch their own food within a day of hatching.

DATE AND LOCATION SEEN: ______________________

____

____

Chukar

Gray Partridge

DESCRIPTION: 36 cm/32 cm, wingspan 51 cm/48 cm. Medium-size, chunky introduced game birds of dry, open areas. CHUKAR: Male and female alike. Pale grey overall, with **cream-coloured face and throat outlined in black**; short, red bill and legs. **Bold dark barring on buffy flanks**, buffy belly, pale cinnamon undertail, short **rufous tail**. GRAY: **Greyish-brown** overall, with **rufous face** (female's is buff), **bold rufous bars** and pale streaks **on flanks**, grey bill, short rufous tail. Male has **chestnut belly patch**, absent on female.

SIMILAR SPECIES: Dusky Grouse (p. 75) larger, less distinctively marked; lacks rusty tail feathers.

VOICE: CHUKAR: Call is *chucka-chucka-chucka* series. GRAY: Call is hoarse *keeeah*.

WHERE TO FIND: CHUKAR: Fairly common but local resident of arid, rocky foothills and cliffs; especially Thompson Valley west of Kamloops, Fraser Valley from Lytton to Lillooet and south Okanagan Valley. Partial to haystacks and feedlots near rocky habitats in winter. GRAY: Uncommon, secretive resident of farmlands and adjacent grassy uplands in Okanagan Valley, especially Head-of-the-Lake, Vernon Commonage, White Lake, and Chopaka.

BEHAVIOUR: Both species gregarious; post-breeding flocks forage within their respective habitats. CHUKAR: Diet is mainly leaves and insects in summer, grass and forb seeds in winter. GRAY: Eats seeds, waste grain, leaves, and insects.

DID YOU KNOW? Both natives of Eurasia, the first Chukars were introduced to North America in 1893, and the release of Gray Partridges first began in the early 1900s.

DATE AND LOCATION SEEN: ______________________________

____

____

Male

Female

DESCRIPTION: 21–89 cm, wingspan 79 cm. Medium-sized game bird with a **long, pointed tail**. Male is strikingly mottled brown, with dark-spotted, orange flanks, pale-spotted rust back, grey rump, **broad, white neck ring, iridescent green head,** and **red facial skin**. Female is mottled brown with a long tail.

SIMILAR SPECIES: Smaller Sharp-tailed Grouse (p. 73) has a shorter tail, prominent white wing spots, and white tail base.

VOICE: Males give loud, harsh cackle *uurk-iik*, issued in long, rapid series when flushed.

WHERE TO FIND: Fairly common introduced resident of low-elevation southern valleys. Typically found in cropland, marshes, and pastures interspersed with or adjacent to dense cover with water. Most easily found in the Okanagan Valley.

BEHAVIOUR: Forages for insects, seeds, agricultural grains, and other foods. Generally runs from intruders into protective cover, but a strong flyer when flushed. Nests on the ground in tall vegetation. Often forms sizeable post-breeding flocks.

DID YOU KNOW? Pheasants were first introduced to the region in the late 1800s in the Creston area.

DATE AND LOCATION SEEN: ______________________

____

____

DESCRIPTION: 46 cm. Slender forest grouse. **Mottled** and spotted **brownish-grey** all over, with **bold, dark vertical bars on flanks**. Finely barred **tail has wide, dark band near tip**, is relatively long and somewhat rounded. **Head is crested**, though crest is sometimes flattened. Males have large, **dark neck ruffs** exposed when displaying during breeding season, inconspicuous at other times.

SIMILAR SPECIES: Larger Dusky Grouse (p. 75) has solid black tail, sometimes with dark grey band at the tip. Smaller Spruce Grouse (p. 75) has an all-dark tail.

VOICE: Nasal squeals, clucks.

WHERE TO FIND: Fairly common resident of moist deciduous and mixed forests with dense understories, especially riparian areas.

BEHAVIOUR: Mostly feeds on buds and other plant materials, lesser amounts of insects and other invertebrates. "Drumming" male produces low-pitched, accelerating wingbeat sounds during spring breeding display, usually from atop a log. Males also erect crest and neck ruff, fan tail when displaying. Nests on the ground, usually at the base of a tree or stump. Family groups often seen feeding along forest roadways. Female aggressively defends brood with an elaborate distraction display. Usually solitary in winter.

DID YOU KNOW? Like most grouse, Ruffed Grouse are promiscuous; males may breed with several females attracted to their drumming. After copulation, the females incubate the eggs and raise the young without any assistance from the male.

DATE AND LOCATION SEEN: ______________________

____

____

Sharp-tailed Grouse

Tympanuchus phasianellus

DESCRIPTION: 43 cm, wingspan 64 cm. **Medium-sized grouse**, **upper parts** and breast **mottled brown with white spots**; **underparts pale with dark chevrons on flanks**; **head is slightly crested**; **short**, **pointed tail** has white base. Displaying male shows yellowish eyebrows and pinkish-purple air sacs on sides of neck.

SIMILAR SPECIES: Only grouse in region with pointed tail; female pheasant is larger and lacks white on tail.

VOICE: Displaying males produce high-pitched hoots; both sexes give clucking calls.

WHERE TO FIND: Residents of open, upland areas. Rare in grassland and shrub habitats, including logging clearcuts, in Cariboo-Chilcotin plateau and Thompson and Nicola valleys.

BEHAVIOUR: Forages for plant materials and insects. Males gather at leks each spring (March–May) to perform elaborate courtship displays.

DID YOU KNOW? The Sharp-tailed Grouse is declining in numbers across its geographic range, primarily because of habitat loss and degradation.

DATE AND LOCATION SEEN: ____________________

____

____

Dusky Grouse
Male
Dusky Grouse
Female
Spruce Grouse
Male
Spruce Grouse
Female

Dendragapus obscurus / Falcipennis canadensis

DESCRIPTION: 51 cm/41 cm, wingspan 66 cm/56 cm. DUSKY: Large, long-necked, and long-tailed. Male is **sooty-brown above and bluish-grey below** with pale spotting on flanks and belly; **yellow combs above eyes**; **tail is all black or with indistinct grey band at tip**. Smaller female mottled grey-brown with pale spots on flanks and belly. SPRUCE: Medium-sized, stocky, short-necked, and short-tailed. Male dark-barred brown above, **black below with prominent white spots on flanks and belly**. Eyes have **red combs above and white arcs below. Tail black**. Female rufous-brown, with dark barring on brown and white underparts, dark tail.

SIMILAR SPECIES: Ruffed Grouse (p. 71) has prominent, broad tail bands. Sooty Grouse (very similar to Dusky Grouse, which it replaces at western boundary of region) has prominent grey band on tip of tail; male has yellow (not red) air sacs inflated during display.

VOICE: Both species cluck. Male Dusky Grouse give single low *Oop* as well as a series of very low (almost inaudible) *oo-oo-oo* calls while inflating neck sacs in display. Male Spruce Grouse produce distinctive double-clap with wings in display.

WHERE TO FIND: DUSKY: Uncommon resident of coniferous forests and grasslands. SPRUCE: Resident in subalpine forests.

BEHAVIOUR: Both forage on ground for plant material and insects. Spruce Grouse sit in spruce trees for long periods in winter, eating needles.

DID YOU KNOW? Spruce Grouse are often called "fool hens" because they seem unafraid of humans and will continue to feed or display while people stand over them.

DATE AND LOCATION SEEN: ______________________

____

____

White-tailed Ptarmigan
Spring

White-tailed Ptarmigan
Winter

White-tailed Ptarmigan
Summer

DESCRIPTION: 32 cm. **Small** alpine grouse with heavily feathered feet. In summer, **mottled grey and black** all over, spotted with tan; wings white. **White tail** is usually hidden under long coverts. In winter, plumage is **entirely white**.

SIMILAR SPECIES: Larger Willow Ptarmigan (rare in northern Rockies and Chilcotin Range) has black tail in both winter and summer (usually hidden under coverts), rich brown overall plumage (not greyish) in summer.

VOICE: Various clucks; territorial male gives *kik kik kik kikEEYA* call.

WHERE TO FIND: Fairly common but usually inconspicuous resident of high, rocky, treeless alpine areas. Plumage is so cryptic that ptarmigan are difficult to see unless they move, but they generally allow close approach. Some descend into subalpine forests in winter.

BEHAVIOUR: Mostly feeds on willow buds and other plant materials, smaller amounts of insects and other invertebrates. Males and females defend territories in summer, and, unusual for grouse, form strong monogamous pair bonds.

DID YOU KNOW? In winter, White-tailed Ptarmigan can spend most of the day in snow tunnel roosts, especially if the weather is unfavourable.

DATE AND LOCATION SEEN: ______________________

____

____

Male

Female

DESCRIPTION: 91–119 cm, wingspan 127–163 cm. **Large**, familiar forest bird. MALE: **Overall dark**, wings barred black and white; **head and neck skin bluish-grey with numerous pink wattles**; long, black beard projects from breast; rump and tail feathers tipped with buff or whitish; legs are pink, stout; bill short and down-curved. FEMALE and IMMATURE: Smaller; dark plumage tipped buff or whitish; has short beard or none; head has short feathers and small, dull wattles.

SIMILAR SPECIES: Domestic turkey is usually larger, plumper, often entirely white.

VOICE: Displaying male gives familiar descending gobble, females give *tuk* and series of *yike* calls.

WHERE TO FIND: Introduced locally common resident, mostly in lower elevation foothills and mountains of the Kootenay region and Kettle Valley. Populations continue to expand westward to the Okanagan. Usually found in open coniferous, deciduous, or mixed shrub/grassland habitats with water nearby.

BEHAVIOUR: Forages on ground (often by scratching) for seeds, nuts, fruit, and insects. Rarely flies, except to roost in trees at night. In breeding display, male puffs out feathers, spreads tail, swells facial wattles, droops wings, and gobbles. Nomadic and gregarious after breeding season, they often gather in large flocks in fall and move to lower elevation areas.

DID YOU KNOW? Wild Turkey, native to eastern North America, was introduced as a game bird to the western United States; local populations have spread north and are continuing to expand.

DATE AND LOCATION SEEN: ______________________________

____

____

Male
Female

DESCRIPTION: 25 cm. Plump grey game bird with short, rounded wings, grey tail, small black bill, and **curved black topknot**. **Belly is scaled with white**, brown flanks with white streaks. Male has **black throat outlined in white**; dark brown crown; conspicuous flared, forward-curved topknot; dark chestnut belly patch. Female has grey-brown head with little patterning; topknot is small, nearly straight.

SIMILAR SPECIES: Unmistakable in region.

VOICE: Males' assembly call is a loud *chi-CA-go*; courting males give single *cow*; agitated birds call *spwik wik wiw*.

WHERE TO FIND: Abundant at lower elevations in Okanagan and Similkameen Valleys, common in Kettle Valley, uncommon around Shuswap Lake.

BEHAVIOUR: Forages for seeds and other plant material and insects. Gregarious, forms flocks in non-breeding season. Aggressively defends territories and young.

DID YOU KNOW? Although introduced from California and Oregon, populations in Okanagan Valley are likely the densest in the world.

DATE AND LOCATION SEEN: ______________________

____

____

Yellow-billed Loon
Common Loon
Non-breeding
Common Loon
Breeding

DESCRIPTION: 81 cm/89 cm, wingspan 117 cm/124 cm. COMMON: **Large loon**, with a **straight**, **heavy bill**. NON-BREEDING: Grey-brown above, white below. **White partial collar** with broad, dark collar; white arcs around eyes, bill grey with **dark tip**. BREEDING: Green-glossed **black head and bill**; collar of white vertical bars; **black-and-white checkered back**. YELLOW-BILLED: Similar to Common but larger; bill has straight upper and upturned lower; bill generally yellowish with **pale tip**. NON-BREEDING: Pale brown upperparts, brown ear patch on a paler face. Juveniles with pale barring on back. BREEDING: Similar to Common but with massive yellow bill.

SIMILAR SPECIES: Smaller Pacific Loon (p. 85) has relatively small, straight bill; very different head pattern when breeding. Red-throated Loon (very rare in region) is smaller, with distinctly uptilted bill; different breeding plumage; pale grey, speckled in fall and winter.

VOICE: COMMON: Distinctive, low yodels and cries, especially on breeding lakes. YELLOW-BILLED: Generally silent in region.

WHERE TO FIND: COMMON: Fairly common migrant and summer resident (April–September) on lakes throughout region; uncommon in winter on southern lakes. YELLOW-BILLED: Rare migrant (October–June) and winter resident on ice-free lakes.

BEHAVIOUR: Both make long dives for fish. Commons require secluded lakes with good supply of small fish for breeding. Build mound nests on shorelines or islands; aggressively defend territory.

DID YOU KNOW? On land loons walk very awkwardly and cannot take flight at all.

DATE AND LOCATION SEEN: ______________________

____

____

Non-breeding
Breeding

PACIFIC LOON
Gavia pacifica

DESCRIPTION: 64 cm, wingspan 91 cm. Medium-sized loon with straight bill. NON-BREEDING: Dark brown upperparts, crown and **neck sides contrast sharply with white throat** and underparts. Juveniles barred with grey above and paler grey hindneck. Most show thin, dusky chin strap. BREEDING: **Hindneck pale grey**, **black throat**. Checkered **white patches on back**.

SIMILAR SPECIES: Smaller, paler Red-throated Loon (rare) has thin, upturned bill. Common Loon (p. 83) is larger with proportionately larger bill; shows less contrast in non-breeding plumage.

VOICE: Generally silent in region.

WHERE TO FIND: Rare migrant (April–May, October–November) on lakes.

BEHAVIOUR: Makes long dives for fish.

DID YOU KNOW? The Pacific Loon was once considered conspecific with the slightly larger Arctic Loon of Eurasia.

DATE AND LOCATION SEEN: ______________________

____

____

Non-breeding

Breeding

Pied-billed Grebe
Podilymbus podiceps

DESCRIPTION: 33 cm. Small diving bird with a **short**, **thick**, **chicken-like bill**. Plain tawny brown all over. BREEDING: Has black throat patch, **whitish bill with black ring near tip**. NON-BREEDING ADULT AND IMMATURE: Bill is plain pale brownish. Like most young grebes, juveniles and downy young have black-and-white striped faces.

SIMILAR SPECIES: Eared Grebe (p. 91) has longer, slimmer neck, thin bill, and more contrasting grey and white plumage in winter. Horned Grebe (p. 89) has white cheeks in winter. American Coot (p. 127) is slate grey with a black head and white bill.

VOICE: Vocal in summer. Male's song is loud *kuh kuh kuh kow kow kow kow-ah kow-ah*, etc. during breeding season.

WHERE TO FIND: Fairly common migrant (March–April, September–October) and summer resident, uncommon at northern end of region. Uncommon to fairly common winter resident on southern, ice-free lakes.

BEHAVIOUR: Dives for fish and aquatic invertebrates. Forages and nests on water bodies with cattails and other aquatic vegetation. Nest is a well-concealed floating platform attached to emergent vegetation. Seen in pairs or family groups, seldom in flocks.

DID YOU KNOW? When disturbed, Pied-billed Grebes slowly sink their bodies and then move quickly away from the source of danger under water, or with just their heads above water like submarine periscopes.

DATE AND LOCATION SEEN: ____________________

____

____

Horned Grebe
Non-breeding

Horned Grebe
Breeding

Red-necked Grebe
Non-breeding

Red-necked Grebe
Breeding

Horned Grebe / Red-necked Grebe

Podiceps auritus / Podiceps grisegena

DESCRIPTION: 36 cm/46 cm, wingspan 46 cm/61 cm. HORNED: Small, compact water bird with **relatively flat crown**. Has **short, thick neck**, red eyes, **straight bill** with light tip, white underparts. BREEDING: **Black head with prominent yellow eye patch**, **rufous neck** and flanks. NON-BREEDING: Dark grey crown, hindneck, and back; **white cheeks**, **throat**, **and foreneck**. RED-NECKED: **Large** greyish-brown grebe. Wedge-shaped head with dark eyes, long and stout yellowish bill, thick neck, white underparts. BREEDING: **Black crown**, **whitish cheeks**, **rufous neck**. NON-BREEDING: Dark crown and back, dingy pale grey and white cheeks and neck.

SIMILAR SPECIES: Winter Eared Grebe (p. 91) rides higher in water than Horned, has rounded crown, dusky neck, greyish cheek patch and large "behind." Western Grebe (p. 93) is larger than Red-necked; has long, white neck.

VOICE: HORNED: Call is *way-err*; song is trilling and squeaky. RED-NECKED: Call is sharp *krik*; song is loud and braying.

WHERE TO FIND: Both are fairly common migrants (April–May, October–November), uncommon to locally common in winter on large, ice-free lakes in southern valleys. HORNED: Uncommon summer resident on small plateau lakes. RED-NECKED: Fairly common summer resident on marshy lakes throughout region.

BEHAVIOUR: Both species dive under water for small fish and a variety of aquatic invertebrates. Nest on open marshes, ponds, or lakes edged with aquatic vegetation. Build floating nests on aquatic vegetation.

DID YOU KNOW? Both species perform elaborate breeding displays.

DATE AND LOCATION SEEN: ______________________

____

____

Non-breeding

Breeding

Eared Grebe

Podiceps nigricollis

DESCRIPTION: 33 cm. Small, **slim-necked** grebe with a **thin, slightly upturned bill** and bright red eyes. Feathering at the rear usually fluffed out when the bird is resting on the water. NON-BREEDING: Grey above and whitish with grey mottling below. **Peaked crown** is dark down to the cheek; the neck is variably washed with grey-brown. BREEDING: **Head and neck are black** with yellow plumes on the sides of the face. Breast and flanks are chestnut.

SIMILAR SPECIES: Horned Grebe (p. 89) in non-breeding plumage has a flat, black crown, shorter neck with a clean, white foreneck, pale spot in front of the eye, and pale-tipped bill. In breeding plumage Horned Grebe has a brown neck and yellow plume more toward the top of the head.

VOICE: Song is high repeated whistle *ooEEK*.

WHERE TO FIND: Locally common summer resident, primarily in Cariboo-Chilcotin but also on other lakes with rich marshes. Uncommon migrant (April–May, August–October) elsewhere in the region, very rare in winter on larger lakes.

BEHAVIOUR: Dives for small fish and aquatic invertebrates. Nests in colonies on shallow vegetated ponds and lake margins. Like most of the region's grebes, they are rarely seen in flight.

DID YOU KNOW? The Eared Grebe is the most abundant grebe in the world.

DATE AND LOCATION SEEN: ____________________

____

____

DESCRIPTION: 64 cm. Largest grebe, with long slender neck and bright red eyes. **Grey above, white foreneck and underparts**, with **black crown**. **Dull yellow to olive bill**; **black crown extends over eyes** (patch surrounding eye fades to grey in winter).

SIMILAR SPECIES: Clark's Grebe (rare) has schoolbus-yellow-orange bill; eye surrounded by white. Smaller Horned Grebe (p. 89) has much shorter neck.

VOICE: Loud, grating *kree-kreeek*.

WHERE TO FIND: Common migrant (April, October), local summer resident at colony sites, uncommon to rare in winter on southern ice-free lakes. Breeding colonies at Salmon Arm, north end of Okanagan Lake, and Duck Lake, Creston.

BEHAVIOUR: Dives for fish in large marshes and lakes. Displaying birds rush along water surface with graceful, curved necks. Floating nests are anchored to vegetation in marshy pond borders. As in all grebes, downy chicks may ride on backs of parents.

DID YOU KNOW? Western and Clark's Grebes were formerly considered different plumage morphs of a single species.

DATE AND LOCATION SEEN: ______________________

____

____

DESCRIPTION: 127 cm, wingspan 274 cm. **Enormous white water bird** with **long yellowish-orange bill and expandable throat pouch**. Wings long with **black flight feathers**. Legs orange, feet webbed; has short white tail. Breeding adults have small horn on upper bill. Immature: Like adults, except greyish on head and back.

SIMILAR SPECIES: Much smaller Snow Goose (p. 27) has small, dark bill. Swans have all-white wings and dark bills.

VOICE: Generally silent.

WHERE TO FIND: Rare migrant (April–May, September–October) and very local summer resident with a tendency to wander. Only BC breeding colony at Stum Lake north of Alexis Creek. Non-breeding flocks commonly seen in summer at Creston, Salmon Arm, Tachick Lake, and Nulki Lake, and occasionally elsewhere in region.

BEHAVIOUR: Highly gregarious. Forages for fish in shallow lakes, marshes, rivers. Adult often flies long distances daily between nesting grounds and feeding areas. Eats between 20–40 percent of its weight in fish each day. Requires an undisturbed island and reliable source of abundant fish for nesting. Shy and sensitive at nest sites, prone to abandon nest if disturbed. Flocks often seen flying in formation high overhead.

DID YOU KNOW? American White Pelicans often feed co-operatively. Flocks encircle fish or drive them into the shallows, then simultaneously dip their heads and scoop up the concentrated fish with their bill pouches.

DATE AND LOCATION SEEN: ______________________

____

____

Adult
Immature

DESCRIPTION: 84 cm, wingspan 132 cm. Large, with **conspicuous bare yellow or orange skin on face and chin**, **thick neck**, relatively long wings. ADULT: **Black head**, **neck**, **underparts**; scaled above with grey and black. Bright orange-yellow skin in front of eyes and bare throat pouch. Breeding birds have white (or black and white) double-crest plumes. IMMATURE: Varies from **brown to almost whitish on neck and breast**; belly darker; **bare face skin yellow**.

SIMILAR SPECIES: In flight, can be mistaken for geese, which are lighter-coloured and have different flight. Common Loon (p. 83) is heavier, with thick, short neck and pointed bill.

VOICE: Generally silent.

WHERE TO FIND: Uncommon to rare migrant (February–April, September–November) and local summer resident of large marshes, lakes, and rivers. Breeding colonies at Creston and Stum Lake.

BEHAVIOUR: Double-crested Cormorants pursue fish underwater; at surface they ride low in water with bills angled upward. Often seen perched on shore, rocks, or in trees with wings spread to dry. Form colonies; build stick nests in trees.

DID YOU KNOW? This species is increasing in numbers throughout its inland range, but declining on the BC coast because of increasing Bald Eagle harassment at colonies.

DATE AND LOCATION SEEN: ______________________________

____

____

DESCRIPTION: 71 cm, wingspan 107 cm. Large, heavy-bodied wading bird with rich brown upperparts, **boldly streaked brown underparts**, a **black stripe on side of neck**, and green legs. **Dark flight feathers contrast with the brown upperparts** in flight.

SIMILAR SPECIES: Immature Black-crowned Night-heron (very rare in region) has blurry streaks on underparts, lacks black stripe on side of neck, and has rounder, even-coloured wings.

VOICE: Flight call is nasal *squark*; song is deep, repeating *LOONK-Aloonk*.

WHERE TO FIND: Rare and local summer resident (March–October) of low- to mid-elevation wetlands. Good locations include Creston Valley; Swan Lake, Vernon; and Scout Island, Williams Lake.

BEHAVIOUR: Forages for aquatic invertebrates and small vertebrates in wetlands with tall, emergent vegetation. Captures prey using stealth by standing motionless for long periods of time. Most active in early morning and late evening. Frequently calls at night during the breeding season. Shy and secretive, they hide from intruders by extending their necks and holding their bills pointed up in a reed-like pose.

DID YOU KNOW? This secretive and cryptically plumaged marsh denizen can be remarkably difficult for birders to see; many more are heard in spring than are seen.

DATE AND LOCATION SEEN: ______________________

____

____

DESCRIPTION: 117 cm, wingspan 183 cm. A **large heron**, the **only heron regularly occurring in the region**. Mostly **grey**, with darker flight feathers. Has **cinnamon or chestnut "thigh" feathering**, strong, dagger-like bill that is mostly yellow, and greyish legs. ADULT: Has **whitish face**, **pale crown**, **long black head plumes**, and plain pale lavender-grey neck. JUVENILE: Has dark crown and much grey streaking on foreneck and breast.

SIMILAR SPECIES: Sandhill Crane (p. 129) flies with shallow wingbeats and an outstretched neck; has solid grey-brown plumage with a red crown.

VOICE: Calls are loud, deep, and harsh, e.g., *RAAANK*.

WHERE TO FIND: Common summer resident, but concentrated near nesting colonies. In the northern part of the region very rare until midsummer; wanders widely after the breeding season. Winters near open water, mainly by larger creeks, rivers and lakes in low-elevation southern valleys.

BEHAVIOUR: Patiently stalks shoreline or shallow water areas for fish, crayfish, frogs, and other prey. Also hunts mice in open fields. Often perches in trees. Nests colonially; builds large stick nests in tall trees. Flies with ponderous wingbeats, usually with neck folded in.

DID YOU KNOW? The breeding population and range of the Great Blue Heron is steadily increasing in the Interior of British Columbia.

DATE AND LOCATION SEEN: ______________________

____

____

DESCRIPTION: 66 cm, wingspan 168 cm. Large raptor-like bird that is **blackish-brown** all over, with a **bare red head** and whitish bill. The **flight feathers of the wings appear pale silvery from below**, contrasting with the darker body and wing linings. Appears small-headed in flight.

SIMILAR SPECIES: Golden Eagle (p. 107) has wings that appear more uniform in colour from below, larger feathered head, and golden-brown hindneck.

VOICE: Silent.

WHERE TO FIND: Common summer resident, migrant (March–April, September–October). Still very rare in northern part of region, but numbers increasing throughout.

BEHAVIOUR: Feeds on carrion, including roadkills, which it locates by sight and smell. Travels long distances searching for food, soaring on slightly uptilted wings and often rocking back and forth in flight. Can be gregarious; gathers in late afternoon in tall trees to roost. Flocks of migrants ride thermal updrafts.

DID YOU KNOW? Turkey Vultures are one of the few bird species with an excellent sense of smell and can detect rotting carrion from kilometres away.

DATE AND LOCATION SEEN: ____________________

DESCRIPTION: 58 cm, wingspan 178 cm. Large, long-winged hawk. Underparts and head mostly white, with a dark mask extending behind eyes, Mostly **white on the head and underparts**, with a **dark mask through the eyes**, and a necklace of dark streaks across the breast; upperparts are blackish-brown; wing linings are white, flight feathers heavily marked with grey below. Juvenile is scaled with buff on the back and wings and has a buffy wash on the breast. Wing tips **extend beyond the end of the tail** at rest; wings held slightly bent in flight.

SIMILAR SPECIES: Some immature Bald Eagles (p. 107) and Red-tailed Hawks (p. 117) can be very white below and have white head with dark facial feathers, but the eagles are larger and stockier and the hawks are smaller with a different wing pattern; both have shorter wings than the Osprey.

VOICE: Calls are short, chirping whistles.

WHERE TO FIND: Fairly common summer resident (March–October) along rivers and larger lakes; **absent in winter**.

BEHAVIOUR: Forages by diving feet first into the water to capture fish, often hovering overhead before diving. Constructs large, bulky stick nests atop dead trees, utility poles, and man-made nest platforms.

DID YOU KNOW? Ospreys have hook-like scales on the soles of their feet, allowing them to easily hold on to slippery fish.

DATE AND LOCATION SEEN: ______________________

____

____

Bald Eagle
Immature

Bald Eagle
Adult

Golden Eagle
Immature

Golden Eagle
Adult

BALD EAGLE / GOLDEN EAGLE

Haliaeetus leucocephalus / Aquila chrysaetos

DESCRIPTION: 79 cm/76 cm, wingspan 203 cm/201 cm. BALD: Adult has **dark brown body** with **white head and tail**. Immature is dark brown with variable white patches on body and wings. GOLDEN: Adult is **dark brown with golden crown and nape**, faintly banded tail. Immature has broad, white tail base, sometimes white wing patches.

SIMILAR SPECIES: Turkey Vulture (p. 103) has tiny, unfeathered head, holds its wings above horizontal while soaring, and has paler flight feathers.

VOICE: Usually silent. Both species make weak, high-pitched calls.

WHERE TO FIND: BALD: Fairly common resident along rivers and large bodies of water, uncommon at northern end of region in winter. GOLDEN: Uncommon permanent resident of canyons, foothills, and mountains.

BEHAVIOUR: BALD: Forages mainly for water birds and fish plucked from the water's surface. American Coots are main food source in winter. Builds large, bulky nests in trees. GOLDEN: Forages over open country for marmots, rabbits, and other small vertebrates; also carrion. Builds large, bulky nests on cliff ledges or in trees.

DID YOU KNOW? Bald Eagle populations were critically endangered by the 1940s, largely due to pesticide residues, ingestion of lead shot, and habitat loss. Since then, conservation efforts have brought about a remarkable recovery of their population.

DATE AND LOCATION SEEN: ______________________________

____

____

Male

Female

DESCRIPTION: 46 cm, wingspan 109 cm. Long-winged, low-flying hawk with a banded tail; always shows a **conspicuous white rump** patch. Small head has owl-like facial disk. In flight, holds wings slightly above horizontal. MALE: **Medium grey head** and upperparts; **whitish below** with some rusty spotting. Has **black wing tips**. FEMALE: Brown, with streaked underparts. JUVENILE: **Brown**; **pale rusty underparts** contrast with the dark head.

SIMILAR SPECIES: Short-eared Owl (p. 201) has wider wings that are not held above horizontal in flight and lacks conspicuous white rump patch. Cooper's Hawk (p. 111) lacks facial disk and white rump patch.

VOICE: Calls include high *eeya* and thin *sseeww*.

WHERE TO FIND: Uncommon summer resident of open habitats. Numbers increase during migration (March–April, August–November). In winter locally common in southern valleys with open grassland and pastures; rare or absent in northern areas.

BEHAVIOUR: Eats mainly voles, also small birds. Usually flies very low and buoyantly over the ground while hunting. Nests on the ground in a stand of tall grasses or other concealing vegetation. Highly nomadic species; population density is relative to prey abundance. Some roost communally on the ground in winter.

DID YOU KNOW? Unlike other hawks, Northern Harriers rely on their acute sense of hearing as well as their keen vision to locate prey. Their low flights over the ground enable them to hear very small prey animals, such as voles.

DATE AND LOCATION SEEN: ______________________

____

____

Sharp-shinned Hawk
Immature

Sharp-shinned Hawk
Adult

Cooper's Hawk
Immature

Cooper's Hawk
Adult

Sharp-shinned Hawk / Cooper's Hawk

Accipiter striatus / Accipiter cooperii

DESCRIPTION: 28 cm/42 cm, wingspan 58 cm/79 cm. Slender brown hawks with long, banded tails and short, rounded wings. SHARP-SHINNED: **Tail tip is squared**. Adult is **slate-grey above**, finely **barred with orange below**. Juvenile is brown above, with some white spots; white underparts have rows of **teardrop-shaped reddish-brown spots**. COOPER'S: **Tail tip is rounded**. Adult has **blackish cap**, dark grey upperparts, fine orange barring below; red eyes. Juvenile is brown above; rows of **thin**, **dark streaks** show on white underparts; has yellow eyes.

SIMILAR SPECIES: Larger Northern Goshawk immature (p. 113) has obvious white eyebrow, uneven barring on tail.

VOICE: SHARP-SHINNED: Call is high, thin series of *kew* notes. COOPER'S: Call is *kek kek kek kek* series.

WHERE TO FIND: SHARP-SHINNED: Uncommon summer resident of dense coniferous forests; fairly common in southern valleys during winter. COOPER'S: Uncommon summer resident of open forests at low elevations; rare in northern part of region. Fairly common winter resident in southern valleys.

BEHAVIOUR: Both feed mainly on small birds; Cooper's also takes small mammals. Hunt by making stealthy approach followed by short bursts of speed to capture prey. Usually build stick nests in trees. Both species are migratory; winter in valleys where small birds are plentiful. Patrol residential areas for birds at feeders.

DID YOU KNOW? Short, rounded wings and relatively long tails give Sharp-shinned and Cooper's Hawks speed and manoeuvrability in dense cover.

DATE AND LOCATION SEEN: ______________________________

____

____

Immature
Adult

Accipiter gentilis

DESCRIPTION: 53 cm, wingspan 104 cm. North America's largest accipiter. ADULT: **large**, **stocky hawk** with **thick**, **white eyebrow bordered by black crown above and dark grey eye-line below**; **solid dark grey upperparts**, very pale grey breast with fine barring; white undertail, **long**, **unevenly banded grey tail**; red eyes. IMMATURE: Speckled brown upperparts; underparts buffy with dense, dark brown streaking; head is pale brown with **bold white eyebrow**; tail unevenly banded dark brown and grey, undertail white with streaking; yellow eyes.

SIMILAR SPECIES: Smaller Cooper's Hawk (p. 111) lacks bold white eyebrow and has straight bands on tail. Gyrfalcon (rare) lacks bold white eyebrow and has longer, more pointed wings, vertical facial mark.

VOICE: Call at nest is loud, strident *kye kye kye* series.

WHERE TO FIND: Uncommon and local resident of mature coniferous and mixed forests. Uncommon and cyclic winter resident of valleys that have open areas interspersed with trees.

BEHAVIOUR: Hunts by perching briefly and watching for prey. Feeds on medium-sized mammals, especially snowshoe hares, and grouse, quail, and pheasant. Prefers mature forests with large trees and open understories for nesting. Fiercely defends nest.

DID YOU KNOW? Northern Goshawks are well adapted for hunting in forests. Their short, powerful wings allow rapid acceleration, and long tail allows for quick manoeuvrability between trees.

DATE AND LOCATION SEEN: ____________________

____

____

Broad-winged Hawk

Swainson's Hawk

Swainson's Hawk

Buteo platypterus / Buteo swainsoni

DESCRIPTION: 38 cm/48 cm, wingspan 88 cm/130 cm. Variably plumaged soaring hawks. BROAD-WINGED: Adult tail boldly **banded black and white**. Light plumaged with whitish underwings; breast orange with orange bars extending to belly. Some mostly blackish. SWAINSON'S: Relatively slender, **pointed wings**; always has **dark breast and light undertail**. Often shows small whitish band on rump. Adult has strongly two-toned wings from below; **white wing linings** contrast with dark flight feathers. Juvenile is mottled dusky and white; usually shows dark whisker mark and chest.

SIMILAR SPECIES: Red-tailed Hawk (p.117) is larger, has different underwing pattern and lacks strongly barred tail of Broad-winged.

VOICE: BROAD-WINGED: High whistled one-pitch call. SWAINSON'S: Long, drawn-out *keeeeeah* scream on breeding territory.

WHERE TO FIND: BROAD-WINGED: Rare summer resident (May–September) on west and east slopes of Rockies; rare migrant elsewhere in region. SWAINSON'S: Common but very local summer resident (April–September) of open grasslands, most easily found around Vernon and east of Osoyoos, rare migrant elsewhere in region.

BEHAVIOUR: BROAD-WINGED: Forages beneath canopy of woodlands and forest. SWAINSON'S: Flies with wings held in shallow V; feeds on large insects and rodents. Migrants may gather into flocks of a hundred birds or more.

DID YOU KNOW? Both species are long-distance migrants; Broad-winged Hawks travel to Central and northern South America, while Swainson's Hawks go even farther, many reaching the grasslands of Argentina.

DATE AND LOCATION SEEN: ______________________

____

____

Immature

Adult

DESCRIPTION: 48 cm, wingspan 124 cm. Most common and widespread large hawk. Bulky and broad-winged with a **broad tail**. Nearly always shows **pale mottling on the sides of the back**. ADULT: Usually with **reddish-orange tail**. Underparts vary from largely buffy with streaks across the belly to reddish-brown or blackish. All but blackest birds show **distinct dark patch along the leading edge of the inner portion of the underwing**. JUVENILE: Most show some white on the breast, dark mottling on the belly, and have a finely barred blackish and grey-brown tail. Many colour morphs exist.

SIMILAR SPECIES: Swainson's Hawk (p.115) has a small bill, soars with pointed, two-toned wings raised above the horizontal, and lacks dark markings along the leading edge of the inner underwing.

VOICE: Typical call is harsh, drawn-out scream; also gives shorter clipped notes.

WHERE TO FIND: Common summer resident and migrant (March–November) in open forests and grasslands throughout region; locally common winter resident in southern valleys, uncommon to rare in winter in northern part of region.

BEHAVIOUR: Hunts meadow voles and other small vertebrates, either from an elevated perch or by soaring overhead. Courting birds fly in tandem with legs dangled; they sometimes make long, aerobatic dives and rolls. Builds stick nests in trees or on cliffs.

DID YOU KNOW? This species was first described from a specimen collected in Jamaica, hence the name *jamaicensis*.

DATE AND LOCATION SEEN: ____________________

____

____

Buteo lagopus

DESCRIPTION: 53 cm, wingspan 135 cm. Large buteo of open country with variable plumage. Commonly has a **white tail with a wide**, **black tip**; pale, streaked breast; **dark belly** and **pale head** with a small bill. In flight, **underwings** are **white with contrasting black wrist patches**. Soars with wings raised above the horizontal.

SIMILAR SPECIES: Red-tailed Hawk (p. 117) lacks prominent black wrist marks, white tail bases, and soars with wings held horizontally.

VOICE: Usually silent.

WHERE TO FIND: Fairly common, but cyclic, migrant and winter resident (October–May). Occupies open grassland areas in southern valleys, mainly rangeland, pastures, airports, and marshes. Creston area and north Okanagan are good sites; very rare in winter at north end of region.

BEHAVIOUR: Primarily feeds on voles and other small rodents. Usually hunts from perch, or by gliding low over the ground and dropping down on prey. Spends considerable time on the ground, but also uses higher perches. Usually found singly or in pairs, but will form large evening communal roosts in winter when prey densities are high.

DID YOU KNOW? The name "Rough-legged" refers to the birds' feathered legs; Rough-legged Hawks are one of only three North American raptors with legs that are completely feathered.

DATE AND LOCATION SEEN: ______________________

____

____

American Kestrel
Male

American Kestrel
Female

Merlin

DESCRIPTION: 25 cm/28 cm, wingspan 53 cm/58 cm. KESTREL: Small, **dainty** falcon with slender, pointed wings, long tail, and buoyant flight. Distinctive **black stripes on sides of white face**. Male has blue-grey wings, **rusty back**, **rusty tail** with black tip; buff below with black spotting. Female is larger, with barred rusty back, wings, and tail; underparts reddish streaked. MERLIN: **Small** but **powerfully built** falcon. **Tail usually banded black on grey**. Wings and back range from grey to sooty brown. Head is **white eyebrow** with no strong markings. Adult males are greyer above than females; all are **streaked below**.

SIMILAR SPECIES: Sharp-shinned Hawk (p.111) has rounded wings, longer tail.

VOICE: KESTREL: Call is series of shrill, rapid *kli* notes. MERLIN: Noisy around nest; loud *keh keh keh* notes.

WHERE TO FIND: KESTREL: Common permanent resident of open country; not present in winter on northern plateaus. MERLIN: Uncommon resident in all treed habitats; most often seen in towns and cities of all sizes; rare in winter at northern end of region.

BEHAVIOUR: KESTREL: Perches on snags, posts, or powerlines and often hovers while hunting insects and small rodents in open meadows and fields. Usually nests in old woodpecker holes in snags. MERLIN: Flies low and swiftly after birds and large insects such as dragonflies. Usually nests in old crow nests.

DID YOU KNOW? Merlins have moved into suburban habitats in dramatic fashion over the past few decades.

DATE AND LOCATION SEEN: ______________________

____

____

Prairie Falcon

Peregrine Falcon

PRAIRIE FALCON/ PEREGRINE FALCON

Falco mexicanus/Falco peregrinus

DESCRIPTION: 41 cm, wingspan 102 cm. Swift, powerful, **crow-sized falcons**. PRAIRIE: **Pale brown above**, **white with brown streaks or spots below**. **Flanks and "wingpits" blackish**; tail pale brown with faint bands. Brown head with white face and throat, distinct brown moustache mark, thin pale eyebrow. PEREGRINE: Adult **slate-grey above**, white to creamy-buff underparts with **black barring on lower breast and belly**. Face has **wide dark grey moustache**. Tail grey with narrow black bars; underwing barred with black. Juvenile is sooty-brown above, heavily streaked below.

SIMILAR SPECIES: Larger Gyrfalcon (rare) usually grey, heavily streaked below, has weak moustache mark.

VOICE: PRAIRIE: Call is harsh *ree kree kree*. PEREGRINE: Call is scolding *ray ray ray*.

WHERE TO FIND: PRAIRIE: Rare permanent resident of dry grasslands, sometimes in alpine areas. Most often seen in the Okanagan and Thompson valleys and dry canyons of the Fraser and Chilcotin rivers. PEREGRINE: Rare, but increasingly permanent resident and migrant.

BEHAVIOUR: PRAIRIE: Hunts over rangeland, pastures, alpine meadows and canyons for small mammals and birds. PEREGRINE: Mainly hunts for birds, including small waterfowl and shorebirds. Both species nest on cliff ledges; and are among the fastest flying birds.

DID YOU KNOW? In other regions, Peregrine Falcons have been attracted to cities, where they use nest boxes on bridges and tall buildings and hunt urban-dwelling birds such as pigeons.

DATE AND LOCATION SEEN: ____________________

Virginia Rail

Sora

DESCRIPTION: 24 cm/22 cm. VIRGINIA RAIL: Small, dark, short-tailed marsh bird that is usually well hidden. Has **long**, **thin**, slightly down-curved **red bill**. Adult has grey face, **bright rusty underparts** with **black-and-white vertical bars on flanks**. Feathers of upperparts are edged rusty. Immature is sooty. SORA: Small, plump marsh bird with **black face**, **stubby yellow bill**. Rusty-brown above, **grey below**. Immature is brown and buff, spotted with white.

SIMILAR SPECIES: Both are distinctive.

VOICE: VIRGINIA RAIL: Male gives hard *gik gik gik gidik gidik gidik gidik* notes followed by accelerating series of low quacks: *wep wep-wepwepweppppprrr*. SORA: A rising *koo-WEE*, usually followed by long, high squealing, descending whinny.

WHERE TO FIND: VIRGINIA RAIL: Common but secretive summer resident in marshes; local and uncommon in unfrozen, spring-fed marshes in winter. Rare north of Thompson-Shuswap. SORA: Common but secretive migrant and summer resident (April–September) in marshes.

BEHAVIOUR: Both walk through marsh vegetation, feeding mainly on aquatic invertebrates, small fish, and seeds. Sometimes feed more openly on mud flats, pond shores, but are usually shy and hidden. Flight appears weak and laboured.

DID YOU KNOW? Rails are indeed "thin as a rail," having a narrow shape and flexible vertebrae adapted for manoeuvring through reeds.

DATE AND LOCATION SEEN: ______________________

____

____

DESCRIPTION: 39 cm. Stocky, **dark-grey** aquatic bird with a **black head and neck**, and **chicken-like**, stout **white bill**. Small white streaks are on undertail sides; wings show white trailing edge in flight. Has small, dark red shield on forehead; thin, dark band near bill tip. Legs are greenish-yellow; **toes are lobed**. JUVENILE: Pale grey below; downy young have bright red head markings.

SIMILAR SPECIES: Pied-billed Grebe (p. 87) is smaller, tawny-brown.

VOICE: Call is clucking *kruk*.

WHERE TO FIND: Common migrant (April–May, September–October) and summer resident, fall concentrations often number in the thousands. Locally abundant in winter on larger lakes such as Okanagan.

BEHAVIOUR: Dives and dabbles for aquatic plants and invertebrates, forages on mud flats, and grazes land adjacent to water. Flies reluctantly, pattering along water surface to get airborne; flight is rapid and a bit unsteady. Nests in marshes, and is aggressively territorial during breeding season.

DID YOU KNOW? Dabbling ducks such as wigeons sometimes pirate aquatic food plants from diving American Coots.

DATE AND LOCATION SEEN: ______________________

____

____

DESCRIPTION: 104-117 cm, wingspan 185-196 cm. Distinctive, tall, wading bird of open fields and grasslands. **Very large**, with long neck and long legs. ADULT: **Entirely grey with red crown**, white cheek patch. Some summer birds stained rusty on body. Bill is dark. Long, drooping wing feathers cover short tail and form characteristic "bustle." JUVENILE: All grey with brownish wash on upperparts; lacking red crown. Neck and legs fully extended in flight.

SIMILAR SPECIES: Smaller Great Blue Heron (p.101) lacks red crown, has yellowish bill, flies with neck folded against body.

VOICE: Call is loud, descending bugle-like roll.

WHERE TO FIND: Uncommon to rare and local summer resident. Common migrant (March–May, September–November), mainly along one flyway that goes up the west side of the south Okanagan Valley, over the Douglas Lake Plateau to Kamloops, on to the Chilcotin Plateau, the Bulkley Valley, then on to breeding grounds near Anchorage, Alaska.

BEHAVIOUR: Omnivores, they forage in open grasslands, meadows, wetlands, and crop fields for plants, invertebrates, mice, and other small vertebrates. In breeding season, adults preen soil into their feathers, staining them rusty as a means of camouflage. Build large nests in open wet meadows and marshes where the birds have unlimited visibility. Congregate in large flocks during migration. Extremely wary, usually do not tolerate humans approaching them.

DID YOU KNOW? Sandhill Cranes perform elaborate and spectacular courtship displays. Paired birds face each other, bow, and then leap repeatedly into the air while calling with wings spread.

DATE AND LOCATION SEEN: ______________________

____

____

Breeding

Non-breeding

DESCRIPTION: 29 cm. Large plover with a **stubby, black bill**. In flight, always shows **prominent white wing stripe, black "arm-pits," white rump** and undertail, and white tail with black barring. BREEDING: Black-and-white spotted back and wings, black face and breast with white border. NON-BREEDING: Brownish-grey upperparts, pale brownish streaked breast and flanks, and white belly. JUVENILE: Resembles winter adult but slightly browner and more neatly spotted with white above.

SIMILAR SPECIES: American Golden-Plover (rare) lacks black "arm-pits," pure white rump, white wing stripe.

VOICE: High, plaintive whistle *plee-oo-EE.*

WHERE TO FIND: Uncommon to rare migrant (April–May, August–October), usually seen as singles or in small groups. Scarcer in spring than fall; most fall migrants in our region are juveniles. Regular at Salmon Arm Bay and other shorebird sites.

BEHAVIOUR: Individuals in flocks spread out widely on mud flats and in plowed fields, usually avoiding each other while feeding. Feeds by sight, typically running short distances and then abruptly stopping to pick or probe for food.

DID YOU KNOW? Black-bellied Plovers are known as Grey Plovers in Great Britain, since they are mostly seen in drab greyish-brown non-breeding plumage.

DATE AND LOCATION SEEN: ______________________

Killdeer

Semipalmated Plover

KILLDEER / SEMIPALMATED PLOVER

Charadrius vociferus / Charadrius semipalmatus

DESCRIPTION: 27 cm/18 cm. KILLDEER: Familiar plover of upland and wetland habitats. Dark brown above with **orange rump and tail base**. Has white underparts with **two black breast bands**. In flight, appears long-tailed, and long wings show white stripe. SEMIPALMATED: Small plover with **dark brown back and complete breast band**. Bill is stubby; legs are yellow or orange. BREEDING: Face and breast band are black; bill has bright orange base. NON-BREEDING: Lacks black areas.

SIMILAR SPECIES: None in region.

VOICE: KILLDEER: Very vociferous. Call is strident *deee, deeyee, tyeeeeeee deew deew, Tewddew.* SEMIPALMATED: Flight song is husky *too-ee, too-ee*; flight call is whistled *chu-WEE.*

WHERE TO FIND: KILLDEER**:** Common summer resident and migrant (February–November), rare and local in winter. SEMIPALMATED: Common to rare migrant (April–May, July–September), rare in summer, occasionally breeds on Chilcotin Plateau.

BEHAVIOUR: Both species forage using run-and-stop behaviour to catch invertebrate prey on mud flats, shorelines. KILLDEER: Uses a variety of other open habitats; nests on gravelly areas, including stream gravel bars, vacant lots, and roadsides. Feigns broken wing to distract intruders approaching nest or young.

DID YOU KNOW? The Killdeer's cryptically coloured, buff and blackish-brown eggs are often virtually indistinguishable from their gravel surroundings.

DATE AND LOCATION SEEN: ______________________

____

____

Black-necked Stilt

American Avocet

Black-necked Stilt / American Avocet

Himantopus mexicanus / Recurvirostra Americana

DESCRIPTION: 36 cm/46 cm. STILT: Large, slender **black and white** shorebird with **extremely long pink to red legs**. **Bill is slender and straight**. Crown and hindneck are black, rump and underparts are white. Male's back is glossy black; breeding birds have buffy wash on breast. Female's back is washed with brown. AVOCET: Large **black and white shorebird** with **long**, **blue-grey legs** and **long**, **thin up-turned bill**. Has white back, black and white wings. **Head and neck** are a **rich tawny colour** (breeding) or greyish (non-breeding).

SIMILAR SPECIES: Unmistakable. Differentiate these species on bill shape, head, neck, and leg colour.

VOICE: STILT: Call is loud, sharp *pleek*, often repeated. AVOCET: Call is high, sharp *kweep*.

WHERE TO FIND: STILT: Very rare summer resident (March–September) in the southern valleys of the Region. AMERICAN AVOCET: Rare and local summer resident (April–November), in the southern portion of the Region north to southern Cariboo Plateau.

BEHAVIOUR: STILT: Forages by picking and probing. AVOCET: Feeds by sweeping curved bill back and forth beneath surface of water. Both species nest colonially and often together on open muddy edges of ponds and lakes.

DID YOU KNOW? Both species are very defensive at nest sites, mobbing approaching intruders with low intimidation flights and loud calls.

DATE AND LOCATION SEEN: ______________________

____

____

Greater Yellowlegs

Lesser Yellowlegs

Greater Yellowlegs / Lesser Yellowlegs

Tringa melanoleuca / Tringa flavipes

DESCRIPTION: 36 cm/27 cm. Both species have **long**, **bright yellow legs** and plain wings; also a mostly white rump and tail seen in flight. GREATER: Rather large shorebird with **long**, **slightly upturned bill that is grey at the base** (except in breeding plumage). Greyish with white spots above, pale below. In breeding plumage, heavily spotted and barred with blackish above and below. Juvenile has distinct streaks on breast. LESSER: Smaller, with **shorter and straighter bill that is always uniformly dark**. Plumage like Greater, but darker grey, especially on breast; less heavily marked in all plumages. Juvenile neck and breast are plainer grey.

SIMILAR SPECIES: Most likely to be confused with each other. Differentiate on bill characteristics, relative size, and calls. Smaller Solitary Sandpiper (p. 139) has prominent white eye-ring and shorter, greenish legs.

VOICE: GREATER: Loud, shrill, three-noted descending whistled *tew-tew-tew*. LESSER: Softer two-note *tu-tu*, often strung together in a series.

WHERE TO FIND: GREATER: Fairly common migrant (March–May, July–October). Uncommon nesting species in sedge meadows and bogs north of Williams Lake, Clearwater, and Banff. LESSER: Uncommon to fairly common spring (April–May), fairly common fall (July–October) migrant. Breeds north of the region.

BEHAVIOUR: Both are active feeders, running about in shallow water to pursue small fish and aquatic invertebrates.

DID YOU KNOW? Greater Yellowlegs is one of the most cold-tolerant shorebirds.

DATE AND LOCATION SEEN: ______________________

____

____

DESCRIPTION: 22 cm. Medium-sized, grey shorebird with fairly long, greenish legs. Dark brownish-grey above with fine white spots, white below, with dusky breast. **Conspicuous white eye-ring**. Tail has white sides with three dark bars and dark central feathers.

SIMILAR SPECIES: Yellowlegs (p. 137) are larger, have white rumps, and, of course, yellow legs.

VOICE: Call is clear *pee-WEET*.

WHERE TO FIND: Uncommon migrant (April–May, August–September) throughout region. As its name suggests, usually seen singly or perhaps in twos or threes, often using very small wetlands. Uncommon summer resident at mountain and plateau muskeg ponds with sedge marshes and wet meadows in northern half of region, rare in southern half.

BEHAVIOUR: Feeds on insects and other invertebrates snatched from vegetation and mud surface around small stagnant ponds and ditches. Nests in old songbird nests in trees, such as those of American Robins and Rusty Blackbirds.

DID YOU KNOW? Only two sandpipers nest in trees: the Solitary Sandpiper and its close Eurasian relative, the Green Sandpiper.

DATE AND LOCATION SEEN: ______________________

____

____

Breeding
Non-breeding

Spotted Sandpiper

Actitis macularia

DESCRIPTION: 19 cm. Distinctive shorebird that exhibits **constant bobbing**, **teetering motion.** Flies with **stiff, shallow wingbeats**. BREEDING: **Heavy black spotting on white underparts**; bill is extensively pink at the base; legs are pinkish-orange. NON-BREEDING: Brown above with white eyebrow. White below, with brownish patches on the sides of the breast. Bill is dark, legs are dull greenish-yellow or flesh-coloured. Has broken white eye-ring.

SIMILAR SPECIES: Larger, darker Solitary Sandpiper (p.139) has longer greenish legs, brownish breast, bold and complete white eye-ring; in flight shows dark underwings and black-and-white barred tail.

VOICE: Call is high whistled notes *peet-weet*.

WHERE TO FIND: Common migrant and summer resident (April–September) in almost any shoreline environment.

BEHAVIOUR: Energetically walks pond, lake, or stream margins to forage, often lunging forward to grab insects. Usually seen in singles or in pairs, may occur in small, loose groups in migration. Distinctive flight consists of intermittent bursts of rapid, shallow wingbeats. Nests at all elevations along grassy edges of streams, ponds, and other water bodies.

DID YOU KNOW? Female Spotted Sandpipers may mate with up to four different males, leaving the males to care for the eggs and chicks.

DATE AND LOCATION SEEN: ______________________

____

____

LONG-BILLED CURLEW

Numenius americanus

DESCRIPTION: 58 cm, wingspan 89 cm. North America's largest shorebird. **Very large**, long-legged, with **long**, **slender**, **down-curved bill**. Upperparts mottled brown. Has plain crown; underparts buffy and subtly streaked; **underwings are bright cinnamon**; has pale grey legs. Immature has shorter bill and is paler.

SIMILAR SPECIES: Whimbrel (rare) has distinct head stripes, lacks cinnamon underwings, and has shorter down-curved bill.

VOICE: Call is loud rising *coooLEE* and descending series of whistles.

WHERE TO FIND: Rare and local to uncommon migrant and summer resident (March–July). Mainly found in dry grasslands, pastures, and agricultural fields with short vegetation in southern valleys; very local breeder farther north in grain fields near Clearwater, Vanderhoof, and McBride. Good sites include Skookumchuck Prairie; the north end of Osoyoos Lake; fields north of Swan Lake, Vernon; Dog Creek area; and Becher's Prairie, Riske Creek.

BEHAVIOUR: Forages for grasshoppers and other invertebrates and small vertebrates in open, upland grasslands. Pairs perform aerial flight displays, and aggressively defend territories, nests, and young. Nest is on the ground and in the open, but well hidden and often adjacent to conspicuous objects, such as a rock or cow dung.

DID YOU KNOW? Female curlews are noticeably larger and longer-billed than the males.

DATE AND LOCATION SEEN: ______________________

____

____

Western Sandpiper
Adult

Western Sandpiper
Juvenile

Semipalmated Sandpiper

WESTERN SANDPIPER / SEMIPALMATED SANDPIPER

Calidris mauri / Calidris pusilla

DESCRIPTION: 17 cm/16 cm. WESTERN: **Blackish legs**; **relatively long bill with slight droop toward fine tip**. NON-BREEDING: Grey-brown above, whitish underneath. BREEDING: Variably rufous on crown, cheeks, and upperparts; breast, sides, flanks marked with dark arrow-shaped spots. JUVENILE: Cleanly marked grey and chestnut above, clean white below (breast is buffy in August). SEMIPALMATED: Very similar to Western, but **shorter and straighter bill**, no bright rufous colouring. NON-BREEDING: Grey-brown above, whitish underneath, breast dusky. BREEDING: Breast streaked with dark brown; back feathers have black centres and tan fringes. JUVENILE: Back scaled in black and tan, white below, breast grey-buff.

SIMILAR SPECIES: Least Sandpiper (p.147) is smaller, is richer brown in colour, has yellow legs.

VOICE: WESTERN: Call is high, scratchy *djeeet*. SEMIPALMATED: Call is short *chewp*.

WHERE TO FIND: Both highly gregarious and often found together. Locally common migrants (April–early May, July–early October), rare in summer. Mud flats at Salmon Arm are a good spot for these and other shorebirds in late summer.

BEHAVIOUR: Both species forage on mud flats, picking and probing for small invertebrates.

DID YOU KNOW? The small *Calidris* sandpipers are collectively known as "peeps."

DATE AND LOCATION SEEN: ______________________________

____

____

DESCRIPTION: 15 cm. Tiny sandpiper. Appears **short-winged** in flight; at rest the tips of the wings (primaries) are not visible on the folded wing. **Bill is short and thin**, slightly arched. NON-BREEDING: **Grey-brown above**, with **brown wash across breast**. **Legs yellowish to dull greenish**. BREEDING: Breast strongly streaked; back feathers have black centres and some rufous fringes. JUVENILE: Rufous fringes to back and wing feathers, variable buffy wash across lightly streaked breast.

SIMILAR SPECIES: Western and Semipalmated Sandpipers (p. 145) have black legs.

VOICE: Call is high trill *treep* or *tree-treep*.

WHERE TO FIND: Common migrant (April–May, July–October), rare in summer; found on muddy edges of marshes, ponds, lakes, and flooded fields.

BEHAVIOUR: Forages on mud flats, picking and probing for small invertebrates. Generally doesn't enter water as larger sandpipers do.

DID YOU KNOW? The Least Sandpiper is the world's smallest sandpiper.

DATE AND LOCATION SEEN: ______________________

____

____

Baird's Sandpiper

Pectoral Sandpiper

Calidris bairdii / Calidris melanotos

DESCRIPTION: 19 cm/22 cm. BAIRD'S: Medium-sized, **buffy sandpiper with very long wings**; stands with horizontal posture; has dark legs. JUVENILE: Grey-brown back and wings have buff-white fringes to feathers, yielding a **scaly appearance above. Breast is strongly washed with buff**, has short, dark streaks on the sides. Adults in breeding plumage are less scaly then juveniles, and have black spotting above. PECTORAL: Similar in structure, but larger than Baird's; **more patterned above, with strong band of streaks across breast; legs are yellowish**.

SIMILAR SPECIES: Smaller juvenile Least and Western Sandpipers (pp. 147 and 145) lack Baird's distinct scaly appearance and very long wings. Pectoral is similar to Least Sandpiper but much larger.

VOICE: BAIRD's: Harsh, dry *kreeeel* call. PECTORAL: Rich *churrk* call.

WHERE TO FIND: Both are uncommon to rare spring (April–May) and rare to common fall migrants (July–September). Pectorals locally common on flooded fields in spring; both common fall migrants at Salmon Arm Bay and other muddy shorelines. Baird's are also often seen above the treeline around alpine lakes in late summer.

BEHAVIOUR: Both feed slowly and deliberately on mud flats and in shallow water, but Baird's often feed well away from water and rarely venture into the dense, marshy vegetation that Pectorals prefer.

DID YOU KNOW? In spring, most Baird's Sandpipers migrate north through the Great Plains. Pectorals mostly migrate north through the Mississippi and Ohio valleys; they are among the world's longest-distance migrants.

DATE AND LOCATION SEEN: ______________________________

____

____

Long-billed Dowitcher
Breeding

Long-billed Dowitcher
Non-breeding

Short-billed Dowitcher
Breeding

Short-billed Dowitcher
Non-breeding

Long-billed Dowitcher / Short-billed Dowitcher

Limnodromus scolopaceus / Limnodromus griseus

DESCRIPTION: 29 cm/46 cm. Both medium-sized shorebirds with **long, straight bills** and **triangular white patch on lower back. Tail finely barred black and white**. LONG-BILLED: Black bars on tail wider than pale bars. NON-BREEDING: Greyish above and across breast, whitish belly. BREEDING: Upperparts mottled, **sides barred with black**. White feather tips. Underparts chestnut-buff. JUVENILE: Similar to non-breeding, but with buffy breast and rusty feather edges on upperparts. Tertials (feathers that lie over wing tips) plain dark grey with pale edges. SHORT-BILLED: NON-BREEDING: white bars on tail equal to or wider than black bars. BREEDING: Belly usually white, **sides spotted with black**. JUVENILE: Similar to non-breeding, but buffier all over, tertials have complex pattern of buff and dark coloration.

SIMILAR SPECIES: Wilson's Snipe (p.153) is strongly striped on head and back, rarely seen on open mud flats.

VOICE: LONG-BILLED: Sharp *keek*, often in rapid series. SHORT-BILLED: soft, rapid *tu-tu-tu*, somewhat like watch alarm sound.

WHERE TO FIND: Both frequent muddy shorelines of ponds, marshes, and lakes. LONG-BILLED: Rare to locally common spring migrant (May), uncommon to locally common fall migrant (July–October). SHORT-BILLED: Rare spring migrant (May), rare to uncommon fall migrant (July–mid-September).

BEHAVIOUR: Both forage for aquatic invertebrates, probing mud with long bills in distinctive, rapid "sewing-machine" motion.

DID YOU KNOW? Sensitive nerve endings on their bills enable dowitchers to capture invertebrates by feel while probing in mud or water.

DATE AND LOCATION SEEN: ______________________

____

____

DESCRIPTION: 27 cm. Stocky, brownish, short-legged shorebird with a **long**, **straight bill**. Crown and face are **striped**, and back has **long**, **creamy-white stripes** (remember—"snipes have stripes" to distinguish this species from the dowitchers). Breast and flanks are dusky barred, contrasting with white belly. **Orange tail** can be conspicuous when bird is flying away.

SIMILAR SPECIES: Dowitchers (p. 151) have a white rump and longer legs; lack head and back stripes.

VOICE: When flushed, gives raspy *scaaip* call. Perched birds give loud display song *kit kit kit*. "Winnowing" males produce eerie low, rising *huhuhuhuhuhuhuhuhuhu* whistled sounds during high overhead flights.

WHERE TO FIND: Common migrant and summer resident (March–October) of marshes and wet meadows. Uncommon and local in winter in spring-fed streams and marshes.

BEHAVIOUR: Secretive, usually hiding motionlessly within short marshy vegetation; flushes with zigzag flight. Sometimes feeds more openly on mud flats, but rarely far from concealing vegetation. Usually found singly, but in good habitat small, loose groups can sometimes be found.

DID YOU KNOW? A male Wilson's Snipe produces winnowing sounds in flight high over a marsh to advertise his territorial ownership and attract a mate. The sound is not produced by his voice, however, but by air flowing over thin, curved outer tail feathers. The feathers are spread at the bottom of shallow dives.

DATE AND LOCATION SEEN: ______________________

Female (Left) and Male (Right)

WILSON'S PHALAROPE
Phalaropus tricolor

DESCRIPTION: 23 cm. Phalaropes are unique swimming sandpipers with lobed toes; females are larger than males and much brighter in breeding plumage. Wilson's is a plump phalarope with **needle-like bill**. In flight, **wings are plain** and **rump is white**. BREEDING: Females have **broad dark-brown stripe through eye and down sides of neck**; hindneck is white and foreneck is apricot; males are similar but duller. NON-BREEDING: Pale greyish above, whitish below. Short greenish-yellow legs. JUVENILE: Dark feathering above has buffy edges; buff wash across front of neck in fresh plumage.

SIMILAR SPECIES: Lesser Yellowlegs (p.137) has longer legs, feeds by wading in shallow water. Smaller Red-necked Phalarope (p. 157) has short, needle-like bill, dark eye patch in non-breeding plumage, wing stripes, dark centred tail.

VOICE: Call is distinctive, low, grunting *wemp*, often given in short series.

WHERE TO FIND: Uncommon migrant and summer resident (April–August) in alkaline lakes and ponds throughout region, mainly in Okanagan, Nicola, Thompson, and Cariboo-Chilcotin areas. Rare and local in the Rockies.

BEHAVIOUR: Swims, spinning rapidly to bring food to surface on shallow marshes or marshy edges of lakes. More likely seen feeding on mud flats than other phalaropes, walking with forward-lunging gait, picking up brine flies, other prey.

DID YOU KNOW? In fall, Wilson's Phalaropes migrate to wetlands in South America, some travelling as far south as Tierra del Fuego.

DATE AND LOCATION SEEN: ____________________

Breeding Female
Juvenile

Red-necked Phalarope
Phalaropus lobatus

DESCRIPTION: 20 cm. Region's smallest phalarope, with a **short, thin bill**, white **wing stripes**, and dark central tail feathers. NON-BREEDING: Has **dark patch through the eye**; **back striped** dark grey and white. BREEDING: Has slate grey crown and face, white patch on sides of throat, red neck sides; sides of breast dark grey, upperparts grey with gold stripes. Females are darker and brighter than males. JUVENILE: Like non-breeding adult, but with dark cap, black and buff upperparts.

SIMILAR SPECIES: Larger Wilson's Phalarope (p. 155) has a prominent white rump. Larger non-breeding Red Phalarope (rare) is pale grey and white with a heavier bill.

VOICE: Call is hard *kett*.

WHERE TO FIND: Uncommon to fairly common migrant (April–May, July–September) with largest numbers staging at alkaline lakes.

BEHAVIOUR: A swimming shorebird that forages for aquatic insects and brine shrimp. Highly social, often forms post-breeding flocks.

DID YOU KNOW? Red-necked Phalaropes often feed by spinning rapidly in tight circles to create upwellings that bring small food items to the water's surface.

DATE AND LOCATION SEEN: ______________________

____

____

Franklin's Gull

Bonaparte's Gull
Breeding

Bonaparte's Gull
Non-breeding

DESCRIPTION: 37 cm/34 cm, wingspan 91 cm/84 cm. FRANKLIN'S: **Small hooded gull**, upperparts ashy grey, wings grey with **white-spotted**, **black wingtips**. NON-BREEDING: Head black behind eyes, bill black. BREEDING: **Head is all black** with **prominent white eye-arcs**; **bill is blood-red coloured with a fine**, **dark subterminal band**. BONAPARTE'S: **Small**, tern-like gull with **slender black bill**, pink legs. NON-BREEDING: White head; **black spot behind eye**. **White triangle on outer wing is bordered behind by black**. BREEDING: **Head is black**.

SIMILAR SPECIES: Smaller Little Gull (very rare) adults have black underwings.

VOICE: FRANKLIN'S: Short, hollow *kowii*. BONAPARTE'S: Low, grating *gerrrr.*

WHERE TO FIND: FRANKLIN'S: Rare migrant; breeds on prairie marshes to east. BONAPARTE'S: Uncommon to locally abundant migrant (April–May, September–November), uncommon summer resident on plateau lakes in northern half of region.

BEHAVIOUR: FRANKLIN'S: Walks plowed farm fields or swims in marshes and other water bodies. Forages for insects, earthworms, and small vertebrates. Nests in marshes. BONAPARTE'S: Plucks small fish or invertebrates from surface of water or plunge dives to capture prey; nest in coniferous trees on islands in lakes.

DID YOU KNOW? Bonaparte's Gulls have a very concentrated spring migration; the bulk of the population moves north through the Okanagan Valley in the last few days of April and the first few days of May.

DATE AND LOCATION SEEN: ______________________

____

____

Ring-billed Gull
Adult

Ring-billed Gull
Immature

Mew Gull
Adult

Mew Gull
Immature

DESCRIPTION: 119 cm/41 cm, wingspan 117 cm/109 cm. Medium-size gulls with **yellowish legs**. RING-BILLED: Breeding adult has **black ring near bill tip and yellowish-white eye**. Non-breeding adult has head and neck flecked with brown. MEW: Adult similar to Ring-billed, but **slightly smaller**. Upperparts **slightly darker grey, eyes dark, bill smaller, yellow with no obvious markings**. Non-breeding adult has head and chest streaked with brown. Immatures of both species brown and grey like most young gulls; bill pink with dark tip.

SIMILAR SPECIES: Adult California Gull (p.163) similar to Ring-billed, but has darker grey back and a black and red spot on yellow bill.

VOICE: Both give high, hoarse cries; Mew Gull's call clearer than Ring-billed.

WHERE TO FIND: RING-BILLED: Common summer resident and migrant (February-November), locally abundant breeder, common in winter around ice-free lakes in southern valleys. Breeding colonies at Osoyoos, Lake Country, Salmon Arm, and Fraser Lake. MEW: Uncommon to rare migrant (April–May, September–October) throughout region, rare winter resident around ice-free lakes in southern valleys. Breeds further north in boreal forest and taiga.

BEHAVIOUR: Omnivorous, they forage in farm fields, bodies of water, landfills, parks, dams, fast-food outlets, and residential areas for invertebrates, small vertebrates, and refuse. Typically make dawn and dusk flights between communal roosts and feeding locations.

DID YOU KNOW? Ring-billed Gulls often eat meadow voles exposed by haying operations.

DATE AND LOCATION SEEN: ______________________________

____

____

Adult
Immature

California Gull
Larus californicus

DESCRIPTION: 53 cm, wingspan 135 cm. Medium-sized gull with pale grey back and wings, black wing tips with white spots, white head and underparts, yellow bill, and **yellowish legs**. Upperparts **slightly darker grey** than other common gulls, **eyes dark**, **bill yellow with red and black spots near tip**. Non-breeding adult has head and chest streaked with brown.

SIMILAR SPECIES: Adult Ring-billed Gull (p.161) is paler grey, has black ring on yellow bill; Mew Gull (p.161) lacks any distinct marking on its small, yellow bill.

VOICE: High, hoarse cries.

WHERE TO FIND: Common migrant (March–April, September–October); uncommon and local summer resident. Common to rare in winter around ice-free southern lakes.

BEHAVIOUR: Omnivorous, foraging in farm fields, bodies of water, landfills, parks, dams, and residential areas for invertebrates, small vertebrates, and refuse. Large numbers gather in late summer and fall at salmon spawning areas.

DID YOU KNOW? The California Gull is the state bird of Utah, honoured as such because the species saved early settlers by consuming hordes of locusts.

DATE AND LOCATION SEEN: ______________________

____

____

Herring Gull
Adult
Herring Gull
Immature
Thayer's Gull
Adult
Thayer's Gull
Immature

HERRING GULL / THAYER'S GULL

Larus argentatus / Larus thayeri

DESCRIPTION: 64/58 cm, wingspan 147/140 cm. **Pink-legged gulls** with **pale grey upperparts**, **black or blackish wing tips**. HERRING: Adult has **limited black in the wing tips**; **eyes are pale yellowish**. In winter, head is streaked and mottled with brown. Immatures are greyish brown with blackish wingtips and tail. THAYER'S: Head is rounded, bill rather small, giving bird "cute" appearance. Adult **wing tips have limited black above, grey below**, **eyes are brown**, legs **bright** pink. Immature is like a small, washed-out version of Herring.

SIMILAR SPECIES: Smaller California Gull (p.163) is slimmer and adults have greenish legs; Glaucous-winged Gull (p. 167) has grey wingtips and brown eyes.

VOICE: Typical gull squeals and cackles.

WHERE TO FIND: HERRING: Common migrant (March–May, September–October) throughout the region and locally common winter resident around ice-free lakes in southern valleys. Locally common around nesting colonies in summer; major colonies at Babine Lake, Bridge Lake, Ootsa Lake, Stuart Lake, Stum Lake, and Trembleur Lake. THAYER'S: Rare to uncommon migrant throughout region; a few winter in southern valleys. Nests in high Arctic.

BEHAVIOUR: Both forage mainly for fish with other gull species at lakes, reservoirs, and rivers, and for urban refuse at landfills.

DID YOU KNOW? The Thayer's Gull was first described by W.S. Brooks, the father of noted Okanagan ornithologist Allan Brooks.

DATE AND LOCATION SEEN: ______________________

____

____

Adult
Immature

Glaucous-winged Gull
Larus glaucescens

DESCRIPTION: 66 cm, wingspan 147 cm. **Large** and stocky Pacific Coast gull with a grey back and wings; white head, tail, and underparts. Has **pink legs**, **dark eyes**, and a long, heavy yellow bill with a red spot. NON-BREEDING: Adult has **extensive pale brownish mottling on head and neck**, **unicoloured light grey back and wings**. First-winter immature is **mottled pale greyish-brown all over** with an all-black bill.

SIMILAR SPECIES: Herring Gull (p. 165) has pale grey upperparts and black wing tips, yellow eyes; Glaucous Gull (rare) is much paler in immature plumages with pink base to bill; adult has white wing tips (not grey). Thayer's Gull (p. 165) is smaller, adult has black wing tips.

VOICE: Typical gull calls.

WHERE TO FIND: Uncommon migrant and winter resident (October–April) along rivers and lakes in southern valleys.

BEHAVIOUR: Forages on large rivers, lakes, and landfills for anything edible. Typically seen with other gulls in winter flocks at reliable feeding locations.

DID YOU KNOW? Glaucous-winged and Western Gulls commonly interbreed.

DATE AND LOCATION SEEN: ______________________

____

____

DESCRIPTION: 53 cm, wingspan 122 cm. Region's largest tern. Has a stout, **deep red bill** and tail slightly forked. Always **blackish underneath the wing tips**. Breeding adult has a black crown, squared at the rear. Upperparts are pale grey, otherwise white. Legs are black.

SIMILAR SPECIES: All other terns are much smaller.

VOICE: Call is deep, harsh *kraa-aay-ow*.

WHERE TO FIND: Uncommon to rare migrant and non-breeding summer resident (April–September) throughout region.

BEHAVIOUR: Makes low foraging flights over water for fish, plunges into water to make catch. Often stands on river bars, mud flats, or lakeshores when not feeding. Frequently wanders in search of reliable food sources after breeding.

DID YOU KNOW? Caspian Terns are the largest, most aggressive, and least gregarious of region's terns.

DATE AND LOCATION SEEN: ____________________

____

____

Forster's Tern
Adult
Forster's Tern
Immature
Common Tern
Adult
Common Tern
Immature

Forster's Tern / Common Tern

Sterna forsteri / Sterna hirundo

DESCRIPTION: 33 cm/30 cm, wingspan 79 cm/76 cm. Medium-sized terns with pale grey upperparts, black crowns (breeding), long, deeply forked white tails. FORSTER'S: Breeding adult has **orange bill** with dark tip, **orange legs**, **silvery-white wings**. Non-breeding adults and immatures have **white crown**, **black patch extending back from eye**, darker flight feathers, black bill. COMMON: Breeding adult has **red bill** with dark tip, **red legs**, pale grey underparts, **grey wings with black wedge on trailing edge**. Non-breeding adults and immatures have **black rear hood**, black or mostly black bill and legs, **dark bar at bend of wing**.

SIMILAR SPECIES: Larger Caspian Tern (p. 169) has thick, red bill; Arctic Tern (rare) has all-red bill without black tip.

VOICE: FORSTER'S: Call is descending *kerrr*. COMMON: Call is harsh *kee-arrr*.

WHERE TO FIND: FORSTER'S: Rare and local breeder; only colony in region is at Duck Lake, Creston. Very rare migrant elsewhere in region. COMMON: Uncommon fall migrant (August–October), rare in spring and summer.

BEHAVIOUR: Both forage for small fish, nest colonially. FORSTER'S: Nests in open-water marshes. COMMON: Nests on islands, but no colonies in region.

DID YOU KNOW? Tern populations were devastated by the millinery trade in the late 19th century.

DATE AND LOCATION SEEN: ______________________________

Adult Breeding
Juvenile

DESCRIPTION: 25 cm, wingspan 61 cm. Small, dark, short-tailed tern. All plumages have **grey wings**, **underwings**, back, and tail. Undertail is white, bill is thin and black. BREEDING: Has mostly **black body**. NON-BREEDING: Adult and immature have white heads with black crown and ear patches, underparts white with dark patches on sides of breast.

SIMILAR SPECIES: All other terns have white underwings, pale grey backs, and are larger.

VOICE: Call is harsh *keff*.

WHERE TO FIND: Common migrant and locally common summer resident (April–September). Good sites include Elizabeth Lake, Cranbrook; Creston Valley; and many Cariboo marshes.

BEHAVIOUR: Diet is mainly insects and other aquatic invertebrates, and small fish. Feeds with buoyant, erratic flight. Flocks swoop to pluck prey from water's surface or by catching insects on the wing. Breeds colonially in wetlands that have dense emergent vegetation and open-water areas.

DID YOU KNOW? Black Tern populations have declined in many areas due to the loss of wetland habitats.

DATE AND LOCATION SEEN: ______________________

____

____

Rock Pigeon

Band-tailed Pigeon

Rock Pigeon / Band-tailed Pigeon

Columba livia / Patagioenas fasciata

DESCRIPTION: 33 cm/37 cm. Large pigeons. ROCK: Quintessential domestic bird of cities and other areas of human habitation. "Wild type" birds are mainly grey with **white rump band, black wing-bars**, **white wing linings**, and iridescent neck sides; tail has black terminal band and white edges. An **array of other plumages** is noted in city flocks, from pure white to reddish-brown or nearly black; many are pied and asymmetrically marked. BAND-TAILED: Large, grey, long-tailed pigeon with **pale band across tip of tail;** bill yellow with black tip, **white crescent on nape**.

SIMILAR SPECIES: No other similar birds in region.

VOICE: ROCK: Gruff cooing notes. BAND-TAILED: Owl-like *hu-woo, hu-woo.*

WHERE TO FIND: ROCK: Common resident of cities and agricultural areas. Colonies often located in canyons or on rock outcrops. BAND-TAILED: Forests along east slope of Coast Mountains (Lillooet, Spences Bridge), at least formerly in the moist forests of the Columbia Mountains.

BEHAVIOUR: Both species forage for grain and seeds in farm fields, will come to feeders. ROCK: Introduced species that nests colonially on cliff faces, usually near agricultural areas where it feeds. In cities and towns or around farms it nests on ledges of buildings or bridges, and other tall structures. BAND-TAILED: Feeds on berries, especially elderberries, in forests and towns, gathers at mineral sources such as warm springs.

DID YOU KNOW? Band-tailed Pigeons need to ingest mineral soils for sodium, an essential nutrient largely lacking in their berry diet.

DATE AND LOCATION SEEN: ______________________

Mourning Dove

Eurasian Collared-Dove

Mourning Dove / Eurasian Collared-Dove

Zenaida macroura / Streptopelia decaoto

DESCRIPTION: 30 cm/33 cm. MOURNING: Slender pale brown dove with **pointed**, **white-edged tail**, black facial spot, and a few **black spots on the wings**. Legs are pink, eye-ring is pale bluish. COLLARED-DOVE: Pale grey-brown with **black hindneck collar** and **dark wing tips**. Has long, broad, **square tail with dark grey base** and white corners, and **grey undertail coverts**.

SIMILAR SPECIES: Ringed Turtle-Dove (a.k.a., African Collared-Dove) is a frequently escaped cage bird and smaller, paler version of Eurasian Collared-Dove that lacks dark wing tips and undertail.

VOICE: MOURNING: Mournful *ooAAH coooo coo coo*. COLLARED-DOVE: Three-syllable hooting *coo COOO cup*.

WHERE TO FIND: MOURNING: Common migrant and summer resident in southern agricultural and suburban areas and ponderosa pine forests; rare in north; does not occur in heavily wooded areas. Locally common in winter near feeders and feedlots in southern half of region, rare in north. COLLARED-DOVE: Local resident of some agricultural and residential areas; population and geographic extent are rapidly expanding. At present, most abundant around Cawston in Similkameen Valley.

BEHAVIOUR: Both forage for seeds on the ground in open habitats. Commonly seen on overhead wires. Except when nesting, both species are gregarious, and form wintering flocks that visit feedlots and farm fields.

DID YOU KNOW? Doves and pigeons feed their nestlings "pigeon milk," a rich, semi-solid secretion formed in their crops.

DATE AND LOCATION SEEN: ______________________

____

____

DESCRIPTION: 41 cm, wingspan 107 cm. Medium-sized, very **pale buffy**, **grey**, **and white** owl with **dark eyes** and **heart-shaped face**. FEMALE: Usually deep buff on underparts. MALE: Underparts all-white. Large rounded head with no "ear" tufts. Appears entirely white at night when flying overhead.

SIMILAR SPECIES: Short-eared owls (p. 201) have dark wing patches, distinctly barred breasts, and moth-like flight.

VOICE: Common call is rasping, hissing screech, often given in flight.

WHERE TO FIND: Rare to locally uncommon resident of Okanagan Valley, especially valley bottom pastures of Oliver-Osoyoos area; rare visitor elsewhere in region.

BEHAVIOUR: Active at night, hunts for rodents with long, coursing flights. Roosts quietly during the day in trees, cutbanks, or structures (barns and outbuildings, haystacks, bridges). Nests in large tree cavities, cutbanks, ledges, old buildings, haystacks, or suitably large nest boxes. Breeding cycle dependent upon prey numbers; can breed any time of year.

DID YOU KNOW? Barn Owls have difficulty catching prey in snowy conditions and begin to starve quickly after a deep, lasting snowfall.

DATE AND LOCATION SEEN: ______________________

____

____

DESCRIPTION: 17 cm. Very small, migratory, **dark-eyed** forest owl. Overall mottled grey with **pale**, **dark**, **and cinnamon highlights**; has **short "ear" tufts** (often not visible) and a **round**, **grey**, **or rusty facial disk**.

SIMILAR SPECIES: Much larger Western Screech-Owl (p. 183) has yellow eyes.

VOICE: Song is low, soft *boop* or *boo-boop* hoots in series.

WHERE TO FIND: Uncommon summer resident of dry, open Douglas-fir and ponderosa pine forests, very rare migrant (May–June, August–October) elsewhere in region. Good locations include Wheeler Mountain, Kamloops; Max Lake, Penticton; Fraser River south of Williams Lake.

BEHAVIOUR: Forages mainly for crickets, moths, beetles, and other insects. Nests in cavities, usually those made by Northern Flickers, also uses nest boxes.

DID YOU KNOW? Until 1977 there were only four records of the Flammulated Owl in Canada, but nocturnal searches since then have greatly expanded our knowledge of its range.

DATE AND LOCATION SEEN: ______________________

DESCRIPTION: 22 cm. **Small** (size of extra-large coffee cup), finely marked brownish-grey woodland owl with **yellow eyes**, short "ear" tufts (often not visible), **white spots on sides of back and wings**. Like most of our owls, it is best detected and identified by voice.

SIMILAR SPECIES: Much smaller Flammulated Owl (p.181) has dark eyes. Northern Saw-whet Owl (p. 203) is smaller, browner, lacks "ear" tufts, has coarsely streaked underparts.

VOICE: Calls include barking, chuckling; song is an accelerating "bouncing ball" series of short, low, hollow whistles: *hoo hoo hoo-hoo-hoo-oo-oo-oo-oo*. Pairs often duet with a double-trill call: *d-d-d, d-d-d-d-d-dr*.

WHERE TO FIND: Rare resident of riparian woodlands with large, mature deciduous trees in southern valleys. Most often reported from the Okanagan Valley and Lillooet area, also found in Similkameen, Kettle, and the southern Kootenay valleys.

BEHAVIOUR: Omnivorous, they perch in likely areas and wait for prey consisting of small rodents, birds, beetles, moths, crickets, crayfish, and other invertebrates. Nest in tree cavities or nest boxes. Nocturnal, they generally occupy daytime roosts in dense tree cover or in tree cavities.

DID YOU KNOW? Screech-Owls don't screech—if you hear a loud screeching at night it is likely a young Great Horned Owl.

DATE AND LOCATION SEEN: ____________________

____

____

GREAT HORNED OWL

Bubo virginianus

DESCRIPTION: 56 cm, wingspan 112 cm. Our familiar **large, tufted** owl. The size of a Red-tailed Hawk, with **yellow eyes**, finely barred and streaked brown, grey and white plumage. Has conspicuous **white throat** collar. Females are larger than males.

SIMILAR SPECIES: Smaller Long-eared Owl (p.199) has longer and more closely spaced "ear" tufts and more streaked underparts.

VOICE: Song is familiar, deep *hoo h'HOOO hoo hoo*. Juvenile begging call is rising, screeching *reeeEK*.

WHERE TO FIND: Common resident of almost all habitats in the region, including residential areas with parks and woodlots.

BEHAVIOUR: Typically hunts at night from perches overlooking open areas. Diet is usually rodents, but can include many other small or medium-sized vertebrates, such as rabbits, skunks, small cats, and other owls. Calling birds often sit conspicuously atop tall trees and utility poles. Nest sites include old stick nests built by other large birds, broken snag tops, cliff ledges, and even buildings.

DID YOU KNOW? Great Horned Owls are surprisingly early breeders, often courting in December and laying eggs in January and February.

DATE AND LOCATION SEEN: ______________________

____

____

DESCRIPTION: 58 cm, wingspan 132 cm. **Large** nomadic, mostly **white owl** with yellow eyes, pure white face, and round head lacking "ear" tufts. MALE: Body is mostly white with faint dark markings all over. FEMALE, IMMATURE: Heavily barred with black on white.

SIMILAR SPECIES: Smaller Barn Owl (p.179) can appear white at night (especially when seen flying overhead), but is tawny brown on upperparts.

VOICE: Mostly silent in winter.

WHERE TO FIND: Rare and irregular winter visitor from the Arctic, most often seen in open areas, e.g., fields, roadsides, airports.

BEHAVIOUR: Opportunistic hunters, they perch on the ground, fence posts, and buildings in open areas, especially near wet meadows and lakeshores where their preferred prey—waterfowl and meadow voles—are abundant. Usually seen during the day, roosting on exposed perches.

DID YOU KNOW? In winters with poor lemming and ptarmigan populations in the Arctic, small numbers of Snowy Owls "irrupt" or migrate to the region in search of food.

DATE AND LOCATION SEEN: ______________________

____

____

DESCRIPTION: 41 cm. Medium-sized, **long-tailed, diurnal** owl. Dark brown above with white spots, white below, heavily barred with brown. Has greyish-white face **boldly framed with black**, yellow eyes and bill.

SIMILAR SPECIES: Distinctive.

VOICE: Territorial song is a long trilled series of hollow whistles, like extended screech-owl trill. Also chirping and screeching calls.

WHERE TO FIND: Uncommon to rare resident of open habitats in mountains and plateaus, usually old burned areas with abundant snags. More often seen in northern parts of the region, irregular in south. Highly nomadic, taking up residence in a territory for two or three years, then moving on. Rare and irregular winter visitor to southern valleys.

BEHAVIOUR: Hunts during the day, specializing in voles, but also taking other small mammals and birds. Only nests where voles are abundant. Nests in natural cavities in snags, large woodpecker holes, and chimney-like tops on broken snags.

DID YOU KNOW? The Northern Hawk Owl gets its name from its daytime hunting habits and its long wings and tail—somewhat like the *Accipiter* hawks and falcons.

DATE AND LOCATION SEEN: ______________________________

____

____

Northern Pygmy-Owl
Glaucidium gnoma

DESCRIPTION: 17 cm. **Very small, long-tailed owl with yellow eyes**. The head is grey-brown with tiny white spots, and **back of head has two black false eye-spots outlined in white**. Upperparts are greyish-brown with pale spots; belly is white with narrow, dark streaking; breast and sides are greyish-brown with tiny white spots, and the tail is narrowly barred dark and white.

SIMILAR SPECIES: Northern Saw-whet Owl (p. 203) is browner, has larger head, shorter tail, lacks eye-spots on the back of its head.

VOICE: Song is series of single whistled toots about two seconds apart: *kook...kook...kook...*; agitated call is a rapid hollow trill: *popopopopopo*.

WHERE TO FIND: Uncommon resident of coniferous and mixed forests. Prefers areas with scattered openings rather than large tracts of unbroken forest.

BEHAVIOUR: A diurnal hunter most active at dawn and dusk, though often seen throughout the day. Hunts for rodents, large insects, and small birds. A swift and aggressive hunter, it readily chases birds in flight or small mammals running on the ground. Nests in woodpecker holes. Commonly makes altitudinal migrations to lower elevations in fall and winter.

DID YOU KNOW? Small birds such as chickadees and nuthatches habitually mob pygmy-owls and can be attracted by an imitation of the owl's call.

DATE AND LOCATION SEEN: ______________________

____

____

DESCRIPTION: 24 cm. Small, **long-legged**, tuft-less owl of open country. The **yellow eyes**, broad white chin, and **white eyebrows** are distinctive. Body plumage is spotted and barred, brown and white. IMMATURE: Has buffy, unmarked underparts.

SIMILAR SPECIES: Much larger Short-eared Owl (p. 201) has boldly streaked underparts.

VOICE: Rasping, rapid barking series *kwik-kwik-kwik*; male's territorial call is *cu-cuuu*.

WHERE TO FIND: Very rare and local summer resident (March-October) of sparsely vegetated open rangelands and pastures, formerly throughout southern part of region but now restricted to release sites south of Kamloops.

BEHAVIOUR: Forages for large insects and small vertebrates. Active in daytime, perching on low, elevated outposts near nest burrow while watching for prey. Perched bird bobs up and down when agitated. Nests in abandoned animal burrows or artificial holes in the ground. Flight is low, with quick flaps and a glide; sometimes hovers.

DID YOU KNOW? Burrowing Owls place animal dung in and around their burrows. One theory about why they do so is that the dung masks the birds' scent from predators such as coyotes or badgers.

DATE AND LOCATION SEEN: ______________________

____

____

DESCRIPTION: 53 cm, wingspan 107 cm. **Medium-sized**, stocky, **round-headed forest owl** with **dark eyes** and **no "ear" tufts**. Upperparts are brownish with pale spots and bars, head is paler. Underparts are whitish with horizontal barring on throat, has **bold vertical brown barring below**, yellowish bill.

SIMILAR SPECIES: Larger Great Gray Owl (p.197) has yellow eyes, distinctive bow tie marking.

VOICE: Territorial call is distinctive *hoo hoo wa-hoo, hoo hoo wa-HOO-aaaaah* ("who cooks for you, who cooks for you all").

WHERE TO FIND: Common resident in moist forests with large trees, especially riparian areas with spruce and cottonwood. Sometimes winters in residential parks and woodlots.

BEHAVIOUR: Forages for mammals, birds and other vertebrates, and large invertebrates. Hunts by sitting in wait for prey, then silently swooping down to capture. Mainly forages at night and roosts during the day in concealing vegetation. Nests in tree cavities and in abandoned nests of other large birds or squirrels. Typically does not flush when approached but remains still and hidden.

DID YOU KNOW? The Barred Owl is an eastern North American species that spread north and westward across the prairies in the early 1900s, reaching northern BC in 1945 then spreading south throughout the region by the 1980s.

DATE AND LOCATION SEEN: ______________________

____

____

DESCRIPTION: 69 cm, wingspan 132 cm. **Very large** owl with **massive round head without "ear" tufts and small yellow eyes. Mottled greyish pattern overall**; face is outlined by **large**, **grey facial disc**, prominent **black and white bow tie** marking on throat. Wings are broad, tail is long and faintly banded.

SIMILAR SPECIES: Smaller Barred Owl (p.195) is browner, has dark eyes, and lacks distinctive white bow tie marking.

VOICE: Low, laboured *hoooaah* hoots in long series.

WHERE TO FIND: Rare and local resident of mature coniferous forests adjacent to wet meadows or pastures.

BEHAVIOUR: Forages by sitting and waiting for prey or by making low reconnaissance flights for voles, pocket gophers, and mice. Hunts by day or night. Often plunges through several inches of snow for rodents detected with sensitive hearing. Uses old stick nests of other large birds, broken off snag tops, or man-made nesting platforms for nests. Makes altitudinal migrations in winter in response to food availability. Sometimes forms loose groups in winter where prey is abundant.

DID YOU KNOW? The Great Gray Owl is the longest North American owl with the largest wingspan, but it is easily outweighed by both Great Horned and Snowy Owls.

DATE AND LOCATION SEEN: ______________________

____

____

DESCRIPTION: 38 cm, wingspan 91 cm. **Medium-sized**, slender owl with **yellow eyes**, **long**, **closely spaced "ear" tufts**, **and tawny-orange facial disc.** Females distinctly darker than males. Upperparts are grey, underparts are mottled brown with **black vertical streaking and barring**. In flight, large tawny-orange patches are visible on outer wings, and prominent black patches near "wrist."

SIMILAR SPECIES: Larger, bulkier Great Horned Owl (p. 185) has horizontal barring on underparts, widely spaced "ear" tufts. Short-eared Owl (p. 201) lacks long "ear" tufts, barred underparts, and is predominantly buff-coloured, not grey-brown.

VOICE: Male gives low, soft *Oooo*. Both sexes produce soft barks, squeals, and mewing calls; also produce loud, single-wing claps in courtship and territorial displays.

WHERE TO FIND: Uncommon and local resident of riparian woodlands, Russian olive thickets, and open coniferous forests, especially those adjacent to grasslands and pastures. Very rare north of Williams Lake and McBride.

BEHAVIOUR: Forages at night for small mammals in open areas and roosts by day in thickets. Typically uses abandoned nests of Black-billed Magpies, American Crows, and hawks for nesting. Forms communal roosts in winter, usually in thickets adjacent to open lowland areas.

DID YOU KNOW? Like some other owls, Long-eared Owls have asymmetrical ear openings that help them locate prey by sound.

DATE AND LOCATION SEEN: ______________________

____

____

Short-eared Owl

Asio flammeus

DESCRIPTION: 38 cm, wingspan 97 cm. **Medium-sized** owl of open country with **round head and yellow eyes.** Short "ear" tufts not usually visible. **Flight is buoyant**, moth-like. Upperparts are mottled brown, underparts are pale with fine streaking. Eyes are surrounded by dark patches. Large **buff patches on outer wings** and **prominent black patches near "wrist"** show in flight.

SIMILAR SPECIES: Female Northern Harrier (p. 109) has smaller head, long tail, white rump, and less buoyant flight. Long-eared Owl (p. 199) is greyer, has long "ear" tufts, rusty facial disc, buffy underwings, smaller wrist patch, and darker belly.

VOICE: Calls include nasal barks and wheezy notes. Male gives rapid *poo-poo-poo-poo-poo* series and claps wings together during breeding display flight.

WHERE TO FIND: Uncommon to rare and local, and declining resident and migrant (March–April, October–November) in grasslands, marshes, and wet meadows. Abundance is highly variable from year to year, depending upon prey population cycles.

BEHAVIOUR: Forages both day and night, usually at dawn and at dusk, mainly for small rodents. Typically flies low over the ground and pounces on prey. Nests and roosts on the ground in high grass or shrubs. Nomadic.

DID YOU KNOW? Short-eared Owls perform spectacular courtship displays, where males fly high into the air above perched females while hooting and rapidly clapping their wings.

DATE AND LOCATION SEEN: ______________________

____

____

Adult
Juvenile

DESCRIPTION: 20 cm. Small owl with **large**, **round head and yellow eyes**. Upperparts brown with white spots on the wings; underparts are white with broad, brown streaks; **face and head have fine**, **white streaks**; short tail.

SIMILAR SPECIES: Boreal Owl (p. 205) is larger, has yellow bill, black outline to face, dark grey cheek patches. Northern Pygmy-Owl (p.191) is diurnal, has smaller head, longer tail, and false eye-spots on the back of the head.

VOICE: Song is rhythmic series of low, whistled *poo poo poo* notes repeated about twice per second. Other vocalizations include nasal, cat-like whines and scratchy barks.

WHERE TO FIND: Uncommon to common, but inconspicuous resident of all forest and woodland habitats. Population densities are highest in mid-elevation coniferous forests. Most easily found in late February through March when males call constantly from treetops.

BEHAVIOUR: Highly nocturnal, usually remains well hidden in dense cover during the day. Hunts at night from low perches. Nests in woodpecker holes, natural cavities, and nest boxes. Many migrate southward or downslope in the fall, sometimes in great numbers.

DID YOU KNOW? Northern Saw-whet Owls are unusual in having asymmetrical skulls; its right ear cavity is large and opens upward, while its left ear cavity is long, narrow, and opens downward. This structure allows them to pinpoint the location of any sound, and means they can catch mice in total darkness.

DATE AND LOCATION SEEN: ______________________

____

____

Adult

Juvenile

DESCRIPTION: 25 cm. Small owl with **large**, **round head and yellow eyes**. Face white with distinct **grey cheek patches;** partially **framed in black; bill yellowish**. Upperparts dark grey-brown with white spots on the wings; underparts are white with broad, dark brown streaks and spots; **forehead with fine white spots**; short tail.

SIMILAR SPECIES: Northern Saw-whet Owl (p. 203) is smaller, browner, has black bill, brownish face. Much smaller Northern Pygmy-Owl (p. 191) is diurnal, has smaller head, longer tail, and false eye-spots on the back of the head.

VOICE: Song is rapid series of about 15 whistled *poo poo poo* notes; the whole series lasts about two seconds. Very similar to sound of winnowing snipe, but rises slightly without falling at end. Other vocalizations include nasal *moo-a* and sharp *skiew*.

WHERE TO FIND: Uncommon, inconspicuous resident of high-elevation forests, particularly mature spruce and subalpine fir. Often near meadows and marshy openings that provide good foraging habitat.

BEHAVIOUR: Nocturnal, remains well hidden in dense forests during the day. Hunts at night from low perches, feeding primarily on voles, but also on other rodents and small birds. Nests in larger woodpecker holes and nest boxes.

DID YOU KNOW? Boreal Owls readily take to nest boxes; in Finland naturalists maintain Boreal Owl nest-box trails much like the bluebird nest-box trails of North America.

DATE AND LOCATION SEEN: ______________________

____

____

Common Nighthawk

Common Poorwill

Common Nighthawk / Common Poorwill

Chordeiles minor / Phalaenoptilus nuttallii

DESCRIPTION: 24 cm/20 cm. NIGHTHAWK: Greyish-brown above, banded brown below; long, narrow **wings with white bands** near wing tips; long, notched tail. Flies with erratic, deep wingbeats, gliding on raised wings. POORWILL: Small, mottled-brown bird with **large**, **flat-topped head and short**, **rounded wings and tail**. Throat black with white band below. **White** (male) or **buffy** (female) **tail corners**. Flight is floppy and moth-like.

SIMILAR SPECIES: When perched, owls look similar but have facial discs and perch vertically.

VOICE: NIGHTHAWK: Call is loud, nasal *beent beent*, and loud, whooshing *Vooom* produced by display dives of males. POORWILL: Call is clear, whistled *poorWILLip*.

WHERE TO FIND: NIGHTHAWK: Common migrant (late May–June, August–September) and summer resident in open areas, less common at northern edge of region. POORWILL: Fairly common migrant and summer resident (April–October) in dry, open, shrubby areas with rocky ledges; north to Williams Lake.

BEHAVIOUR: Both species capture flying insects on the wing. NIGHTHAWK: Makes long foraging flights at dusk, night, and on overcast days. POORWILL: Flies from the ground to capture insects flying overhead. Both roost on bare ground, but nighthawks also roost in trees or on other elevated perches. Both lay eggs on bare ground.

DID YOU KNOW? Both species are members of the nightjar, or goat-sucker, family. The term "goatsucker" originates from an old legend that unfairly accuses this family of drinking the milk of goats at night.

DATE AND LOCATION SEEN: ______________________

____

____

DESCRIPTION: 18 cm. Large swallow-like bird with stiffly held, curved wings. Blackish all over. Tail broad for a swift, often fanned, sometimes slightly notched.

SIMILAR SPECIES: White-throated Swift (p. 213) has contrasting black and white plumage. Vaux's Swift (p. 211) is smaller, shorter-tailed, pale below. Swallows have looser flight on more flexed wings.

VOICE: Call is a series of twittering chips.

WHERE TO FIND: Uncommon migrant and summer resident (May-September) of heavily forested mountains, nests near waterfalls or in shady, moist canyons. On sunny days usually flies around mountain-tops; in valleys more often seen on cool, rainy days. Nests can be seen at Johnson Canyon, Banff; also regular at Swan Lake, Vernon, in late May; and Tachik Lake in June and July.

BEHAVIOUR: Forages for flying insects, especially flying ants, over lakes and mountains; nests on ledges of moist rock walls, usually near, or even behind, waterfalls.

DID YOU KNOW? Black Swifts forage up to 40 kilometres away from the nest, feeding their single, slow-growing young only twice a day. Once the young is more than a month old it is only fed once a day before fledging at 45–50 days of age.

DATE AND LOCATION SEEN: ______________________

____

____

DESCRIPTION: 12 cm. Small aerial bird with rapid wingbeats; often likened to a "cigar with wings." **Dusky**, with **paler greyish throat**, **breast**, and **rump**. Has **short**, **squared tail**.

SIMILAR SPECIES: Larger White-throated Swift (p. 213) has more contrasting black and white plumage, longer tail. Black Swift (p. 209) is larger, long-tailed, all dark. Swallows have looser flight on more flexed wings, usually have contrastingly pale underparts.

VOICE: High, rapid hummingbird-like chipping, accelerating to insect-like trill. Very vocal around roost sites.

WHERE TO FIND: Fairly common migrant (April–May, August–September), uncommon summer resident of old cottonwood groves and mature red cedar forests, sometimes breeds in urban areas.

BEHAVIOUR: Forages for flying insects above the canopy in coniferous forests and along waterways. Nest is a half circle of small twigs glued together with the birds' sticky saliva, placed on inside wall of hollow trees, or less commonly in chimneys. Large numbers roost together at night in hollow trees or in chimneys during migration.

DID YOU KNOW? Vaux's Swift is closely related to the Chimney Swift found in eastern North America; the populations of both species have declined because of declining breeding habitat—large hollow trees and big chimneys.

DATE AND LOCATION SEEN: ______________________

____

____

DESCRIPTION: 17 cm. **Blackish-brown** with **white throat** coming to a point on the lower breast. Has **white flanks and rump-sides**; **long tail** has shallow fork, but **usually appears pointed**. White markings are often difficult to see, but distinctive shape (long, thin wings, elongated rear body and tail) helps to identify it.

SIMILAR SPECIES: Adult Black Swift (p. 209) has no white markings. Violet-green Swallow (p. 275) has different wing and body shape, and different flight. Vaux's Swift (p. 211) is smaller with shorter tail, and is dusky grey below, not white.

VOICE: Call is loud, long, descending series of rapid *jee-jee-jee* notes.

WHERE TO FIND: Common migrant and summer resident (April–September) of rocky cliffs and canyons north to Chilcotin River.

BEHAVIOUR: Nests colonially in cliff face crevices, often with Violet-green Swallows. Forages high over open country for winged insects. Large flocks typically gather in late summer prior to migration.

DID YOU KNOW? The White-throated Swift mating ritual is spectacular. While high in the air, a pair will cling together facing each other with wings pointed in four directions. Then they pinwheel downward in a free fall while copulating, only separating before striking the ground.

DATE AND LOCATION SEEN: ________________________________

Black-chinned Hummingbird Male
Black-chinned Hummingbird Female
Anna's Hummingbird Male
Anna's Hummingbird Female

DESCRIPTION: 9.5 cm/10 cm. BLACK-CHINNED: **Male has black chin with broad purple edge** (usually appears all black), **long bill**, **white spot behind eye**; **broad white collar** below throat; flanks olive; upperparts deep green; tail blackish, slightly forked. Female green above, generally all white below, tail with white corners. ANNA'S: **Male has brilliant rose-red crown and throat**; pale area around eyes; upperparts iridescent green; underparts mostly olive-grey. Female has **small red patch in centre of throat**; underparts **greyish with greenish flanks**; tail corners white.

SIMILAR SPECIES: Female Anna's differentiated from female Calliope (p. 217), Broad-tailed, and Rufous (p. 219) Hummingbirds by greyish breast with green flanks; female Black-chinned from other local hummingbirds by its general lack of buff colour below.

VOICE: BLACK-CHINNED: Call is soft *tiup*. ANNA'S: Call is sharp, high *stit*.

WHERE TO FIND: BLACK-CHINNED: Fairly common summer resident (April–September) of southern valleys, especially riparian areas and gardens. ANNA'S: Very rare summer resident in southern valleys, rare in residential areas in fall and winter.

BEHAVIOUR: Both species forage for flower nectar and insects in valleys. BLACK-CHINNED: Nests in riparian areas and gardens. ANNA'S: A species of residential areas. Both readily visit feeders and flower gardens.

DID YOU KNOW? Anna's Hummingbirds do not migrate; they depend on hummingbird feeders to survive the winter at these latitudes.

DATE AND LOCATION SEEN: ______________________

Male

Female

DESCRIPTION: 8 cm. Region's smallest hummingbird; **short-billed** and **short-tailed**. MALE: **Tiny**; greenish above, pale below, with greenish flanks and **magenta rays on the throat.** FEMALE: Like male except has buff-tinted sides, finely spotted white throat, and **wing tips that extend beyond the tail**.

SIMILAR SPECIES: Very small size, short tail, and lack of extensive rufous in tail of female differentiate this species from the Rufous Hummingbird (p. 219).

VOICE: Produces quiet, very high *chip* notes.

WHERE TO FIND: Summer resident (April–September) in open forests, forest edges, shrub fields, gardens, and riparian areas. Most common in grasslands and ponderosa pine forests; rarer toward north end of region. A few migrants are seen in alpine meadows in July and August.

BEHAVIOUR: Feeds on flower nectar and tiny insects, also visits feeders. Perches and forages closer to the ground than other hummingbird species. Often nests on or near conifer tree cones where nest is well camouflaged. Also nests in riparian thickets. Males put on spectacular U-shaped diving displays, producing a sharp *pt-zing!* sound at the bottom of the dive. Often migrate along mountain ridges.

DID YOU KNOW? The Calliope Hummingbird is the smallest bird in North America.

DATE AND LOCATION SEEN: ______________________

____

____

Male

Female

DESCRIPTION: 9.5 cm. Bill straight, dark. Male's **back**, **tail**, **underparts rusty-orange**; back may have variable amounts of green. Crown green, upper breast white; throat iridescent orange-red. Female's upperparts and crown green; **tail base**, **undertail**, **flanks rufous**; outer tail feathers white-tipped. Red feathering on throat varies from none up to small spot. Immature resembles female.

SIMILAR SPECIES: Male unmistakable. Female Anna's and Black-chinned Hummingbirds (p. 215) show no rufous coloration. Smaller female Calliope Hummingbird (p. 217) has shorter tail with little rufous coloration in it.

VOICE: Both sexes give *chip* calls. Flight feathers of male Rufous produce quiet but distinctive jingling sound in flight.

WHERE TO FIND: Common migrant (April-June, August-September) and summer resident of coniferous forests and gardens.

BEHAVIOUR: Feeds on flower nectar, tree sap, very small insects, and readily accepts sugar water at feeders. Males have distinctive diving courtship displays that are J-shaped, the birds braking at the bottom with a loud *j-j-j-jinngg*!

DID YOU KNOW? Male Rufous Hummingbirds begin their migration to western Mexico in early July, and the adult females follow soon afterward. The young born that year wait another month before flying south on their own in August.

DATE AND LOCATION SEEN: ______________________

____

____

Male

Female

DESCRIPTION: 33 cm. Distinctive, boldly plumaged water bird with a **bushy crown** creating a large-headed appearance. Has a long, dark bill. MALE: **Blue-grey above**, **white below**, with a blue-grey band across the upper breast; white patch on the wings is visible in flight. FEMALE: Similar to male, but with **rusty band across the lower breast**, sides, and flanks.

SIMILAR SPECIES: Other plunge-diving water birds, such as terns, have very different shape and plumage.

VOICE: Loud, staccato rattle usually announces the kingfisher's presence.

WHERE TO FIND: Fairly common summer resident of wetlands, streams, ponds, and lakes. Uncommon and local in winter in low-elevation areas with open water.

BEHAVIOUR: Perches on branches of waterside trees, shrubs, or utility wires. Flies with quick, irregular rowing wingbeats. Hovers over water when foraging, then plunges to catch fish or other aquatic vertebrates and invertebrates. Aggressively defends territory. Nests in long burrows excavated in vertical stream banks and silt bluffs.

DID YOU KNOW? Like raptors, Belted Kingfishers regurgitate undigested fish bones and scales as pellets.

DATE AND LOCATION SEEN: ______________________

____

____

DESCRIPTION: 27 cm. Large, dark woodpecker of open forests. ADULT: **Upperparts are all black** with a greenish gloss. Has broad, **pale-grey collar and breast**. **Underparts are bright pink**. **Dark red face** is framed in black. Distinctive **rowing wingbeats** are crow-like. JUVENILE: Similar to adult, but lacks grey collar and red face.

SIMILAR SPECIES: Smaller Black-backed Woodpecker (p. 233) lacks red face, pale collar, and pinkish underparts.

VOICE: Calls include variety of high-pitched, squeaky notes. Song is series of harsh *chur* notes.

WHERE TO FIND: Fairly common to rare migrant and summer resident (April–September) in southern valleys, mainly in cottonwood riparian woodlands, open ponderosa pine woodland, and occasionally suburban gardens, north to Chilcotin River. Rare in winter in south Okanagan Valley.

BEHAVIOUR: Lewis's Woodpecker has steady, buoyant flight with slow wingbeats and long glides. Mainly forages for winged insects by flycatching. Also stores fruit, berries, and acorns in tree crevices and holes for later consumption. Drills nest cavities into large dead or living trees. Most populations are migratory.

DID YOU KNOW? Lewis's Woodpecker populations are declining throughout their range because of habitat loss and competition from European Starlings for nest sites.

DATE AND LOCATION SEEN: ______________________________

____

____

Male
Female

DESCRIPTION: 23 cm. Region's largest and most distinctive sapsucker. MALE: **Upperparts all-black** with broad, white wing patch, white facial stripes. **Throat is red**, **breast is black**, **belly is yellow**, undertail is white. FEMALE: **Head is brown**; **upperparts finely barred** light and dark brown. **Breast is black**, belly is yellow, flanks and undertail are barred. Both sexes show white rump in flight.

SIMILAR SPECIES: Larger Northern Flicker (p. 235) similar to female Williamson's, but has boldly spotted underparts.

VOICE: Call is harsh *quee-ah*; drums in distinctive series of short drum rolls; *drrt-drrt-drt-t*.

WHERE TO FIND: Uncommon to rare and local migrant and summer resident (March–September) in mid-elevation forests in southern part of region. Highest densities are in mature western larch forests on eastern slopes of south Okanagan and Kettle valleys; also found in larches in southern Rocky Mountain Trench and in spruce-aspen woodlands between Princeton and Kamloops.

BEHAVIOUR: Omnivorous, forages for conifer sap, insects, fruit. Excavates distinctive horizontal rows of small holes in tree trunks and limbs (usually Douglas-firs), returning to eat sap collected in these wells; also gleans carpenter ants from tree trunks and branches. Typically excavates nest cavity in live western larch or aspen with heart rot. Male excavates new nest cavity yearly, but often uses the same tree.

DID YOU KNOW? Williamson's Sapsucker is the only North American woodpecker showing such striking plumage differences between the sexes. Until 1873, males and females were thought to be two different species.

DATE AND LOCATION SEEN: ______________________

____

____

Red-naped Sapsucker

Red-breasted Sapsucker

DESCRIPTION: 22 cm. Mottled black and white woodpeckers that have a **pale yellow belly** and a long white wing patch. RED-NAPED: Male has a **red crown and throat**, black-and-white striped face, **black breast band**, and red nape spot. Female is nearly identical, has small white chinspot. RED-BREASTED: Has **entirely red head and breast** with white at the base of the bill.

SIMILAR SPECIES: Male Williamson's Sapsucker (p. 225) lacks red on the head, has all-black back. Yellow-bellied Sapsucker (rare in northern part of region and on east slope of Rockies) very similar to Red-naped but lacks red nape spot, female has no red on throat.

VOICE: Call of both is mewing *meeah*. Males "drum" in a unique rhythm, often about five rapid taps followed by slowing taps.

WHERE TO FIND: RED-NAPED: Common migrant and summer resident (March–October) of coniferous forests, birch woodlands, and aspen groves throughout most of the region, including both slopes of the Rockies, north to Williams Lake and along Fraser River to Quesnel. RED-BREASTED: Uncommon summer resident in forests of north Cariboo and Fraser Basin. Very rare migrant elsewhere in region, very rare winter visitor in Okanagan Valley.

BEHAVIOUR: Both species forage mainly for sap and insects. Drill distinctive horizontal rows of small holes in tree trunks and limbs, returning to eat sap collected in wells. Excavate nest cavities mainly in live aspens, birches, and sometimes conifers.

DID YOU KNOW? Where the ranges of these two species overlap they often interbreed, creating various combinations of plumages.

DATE AND LOCATION SEEN: ______________________

____

____

Downy Woodpecker
Male
Downy Woodpecker
Female

Hairy Woodpecker
Male

Hairy Woodpecker
Female

Downy Woodpecker / Hairy Woodpecker

Picoides pubescens / Picoides villosus

DESCRIPTION: 17 cm/23 cm. DOWNY: Region's **smallest woodpecker**, with a black-and-white patterned head, **long white back stripe**, white underparts, and white-spotted black wings. **Bill is very short**. Male has red bar on the nape, which female lacks. HAIRY: A larger version of the Downy, with relatively longer and more sturdy bill—about the same length as the rest of the head.

SIMILAR SPECIES: American Three-toed Woodpecker (p. 233) has heavy dark barring on sides, with black barring on a white back stripe.

VOICE: DOWNY: Call is gentle *pik*. HAIRY: Gives a sharper, stronger *peek*. Both also have diagnostic "rattle" calls.

WHERE TO FIND: DOWNY: Uncommon, widespread resident of deciduous woodlands and mixed forests, often in residential areas. HAIRY: Uncommon, widespread resident of mainly coniferous forests.

BEHAVIOUR: Both feed on insects, fruit, and seeds. DOWNY: Forages on smaller trees than Hairy, often acrobatically on outer branches and twigs. HAIRY: Forages on the trunk and larger limbs of large trees; attracted to burned forests, diseased and dying trees.

DID YOU KNOW? Pacific coastal populations of both Hairy and Downy Woodpeckers have a distinctive smoky-grey body coloration, while Interior birds are white.

DATE AND LOCATION SEEN: ______________________

____

____

DESCRIPTION: 23.5 cm. **Black woodpecker with white head and throat, white wing patch**. Male has red nape, which the female lacks.

SIMILAR SPECIES: The only North American woodpecker with a black body and white head; Clark's Nutcracker can act like a woodpecker and has a white head, but has grey body and is much larger.

VOICE: Call is sharp *pitik*; "rattle" call is a loud and extended *peekikikikik*.

WHERE TO FIND: Rare resident in mature, open ponderosa pine woodlands of south Okanagan Valley.

BEHAVIOUR: Excavates nest holes in snags or diseased live trees. Diet is mostly ponderosa pine seeds and insects.

DID YOU KNOW? The White-headed Woodpecker relies on good crops of pine seeds to eat during the winter, and is most common in the Sierra Nevada where several large-seeded pine species occur.

DATE AND LOCATION SEEN: ______________________

____

____

American Three-toed Woodpecker

Black-backed Woodpecker

DESCRIPTION: 22 cm/24 cm. Stocky, medium-sized woodpeckers with white underparts, prominent white moustache marks, and **heavily barred flanks**. Males have **yellow foreheads**. THREE-TOED: Has **variable white barring on back**. BLACK-BACKED: Has **all-black upperparts**.

SIMILAR SPECIES: Downy and Hairy Woodpeckers (p. 229) have white backs and lack heavily barred flanks.

VOICE: THREE-TOED: Call is flat *pik*. BLACK-BACKED: Call is deep *chek* or *chuk*. Both species make "rattle" calls, but are often quiet and inconspicuous. Drum rolls are loud; slower than other small woodpeckers (similar to Pileated).

WHERE TO FIND: THREE-TOED: Uncommon resident of northern and high-elevation southern coniferous forests. BLACK-BACKED: Uncommon resident of mid- to high-elevation coniferous forests. Especially concentrated in areas of recent burns (one to three years after burn) and pockets of bark-beetle infestation.

BEHAVIOUR: Both mostly forage for wood-boring beetle larvae and other insects by flaking conifer tree bark, but may also excavate wood for larvae. Frequently excavate low nest cavities in recently burned trees.

DID YOU KNOW? Both species are attracted to large patches of recently burned or insect-infested conifers, where the two species often occur together.

DATE AND LOCATION SEEN: ______________________

____

____

Yellow-shafted
Red-shafted
Male
Red-shafted
Female

DESCRIPTION: 32 cm. **Large, familiar woodpecker**. Generally **light brown above** with thin, black crossbars and a **white rump**; buffy white with **round**, prominent **black spots below**. Has **black crescent across the chest**. In flight, "Red-shafted" birds show **reddish colour in wings and tail**. Male has red whisker mark.

SIMILAR SPECIES: Unmistakable, but see female Williamson's Sapsucker (p. 225); the sapsucker has shorter bill, yellow belly, and lacks colour in the wings.

VOICE: Call is piercing *keeeew*; also gives muffled *wur-wur-wur* in flight and a *wick-a-wick-a* series. Territorial birds give a long *wik-wik-wik-wik* series, often followed by drumming.

WHERE TO FIND: Common migrant (March–April, September–October) and summer resident across region. Locally common in winter, especially in southern valleys, concentrated in residential neighbourhoods with abundant berries and other suitable food.

BEHAVIOUR: In spring and summer, forages for ants on ground; mostly feeds on berries and other fruit in fall and winter. Flashy wing colour shows prominently in undulating flight. In spring, males often hammer on metallic and wooden objects (often buildings) to create sounding boards for territorial defence.

DID YOU KNOW? Eastern/boreal "Yellow-shafted" and western "Red-shafted" flickers hybridize extensively when their ranges overlap. In the northern half of the region, intermediate birds with "Yellow-shafted" characteristics (yellow wings and tail, black whisker on male, red nape patch) are often seen, especially in winter.

DATE AND LOCATION SEEN: ______________________

DESCRIPTION: 42 cm. Region's largest (**crow-sized**) woodpecker that is long-necked, broad-winged, and long-tailed. **All-black**, with a **bright red crest**, and **black-and-white striped face and neck**; has white underwings and small white patches on upperwings; large chisel-like dark bill. MALE: Has **red crown**, **forecrown**, and **moustache mark**. FEMALE: Same as male, but with **dark forecrown** and **black moustache mark**.

SIMILAR SPECIES: Much larger than all other woodpeckers, pattern is distinctive.

VOICE: Call is series of loud, deep *kuk* notes.

WHERE TO FIND: Uncommon resident of mature coniferous and deciduous forests throughout region.

BEHAVIOUR: Diet is mostly wood-boring insects such as large beetle larvae and carpenter ants. Obtains much of its food from well-decayed snags. Consumes a lot of berries and fruit in fall and winter. Creates diagnostic large rectangular holes in snags while foraging. Nests in large coniferous and deciduous trees, and excavates new nest each year.

DID YOU KNOW? Unlike the circular holes excavated by other woodpeckers, Pileated Woodpecker nest cavities are oval in shape.

DATE AND LOCATION SEEN: ______________________

____

____

Western Wood-pewee

Olive-sided Flycatcher

Western Wood-pewee / Olive-sided Flycatcher

Contopus sordidulus / Contopus cooperi

DESCRIPTION: 16 cm/19 cm. WOOD-PEWEE: Drab, peak-headed flycatcher with **dark olive-grey upperparts**, **dull olive-grey breast**, paler grey throat and undertail. **Wings are long and pointed**, tail is moderately long. Indistinct greyish wing-bars; **no eye-ring**. OLIVE-SIDED: Large, **big-headed** flycatcher with faintly streaked **olive sides** and **white stripe down the centre of the underparts**. Dark olive-grey above; white tufts may show above wings when perched. Wings long and pointed, tail moderately short.

SIMILAR SPECIES: Willow Flycatcher (p. 241) has smaller head, shorter wings, and flicks its tail.

VOICE: WOOD-PEWEE: Call is burry descending *pee-urrrr*; dawn song mixes that call with clear *tee-didip* phrases. OLIVE-SIDED: Call is *pip-pip-pip*; song is loud, "Quick, THREE beers!"

WHERE TO FIND: WOOD-PEWEE: Common migrant and summer resident (May–early September) in open, dry coniferous forests and riparian woodlands. OLIVE-SIDED: Uncommon migrant and summer resident (mid-May–September) of moister coniferous forest edges and clearings, particularly old burns.

BEHAVIOUR: Both perch upright and forage from exposed perches. Make sallies to chase and capture flying insects, often returning to original perch. WOOD-PEWEE: Sallies usually not as long or as high as Olive-sided. OLIVE-SIDED: Wide-ranging sallies from tall tree tops. Both build shallow, camouflaged nests on horizontal limbs.

DID YOU KNOW? Olive-sided Flycatchers favour burned forests, because burns provide open foraging areas, snag perches, and abundant flying-insect populations.

DATE AND LOCATION SEEN: ______________________

____

____

Willow Flycatcher
Alder Flycatcher

Willow Flycatcher / Alder Flycatcher

Empidonax traillii / Empidonax alnorum

DESCRIPTION: 14.5 cm. Virtually identical small flycatchers, best separated from each other by voice. **Upperparts tinged golden-olive** with dull whitish wing-bars and whitish underparts. **Very thin eye-ring** (not obvious) and relatively long, **broad bill**. **Throat whitish**. **Larger and longer-tailed than most other** *Empidonax* flycatchers.

SIMILAR SPECIES: Other *Empidonax* flycatchers have obvious eye-rings; Western Wood-pewee (p. 239) has darker, more peaked head and longer wings.

VOICE: WILLOW: Call is sharp *whit*; song is burry *WITZ-beeer* or *FITZ bew*. Some Willow songs lack the pause in the middle and can be mistaken for Alder songs, but are always accented on the first syllable, not the second. ALDER: Call is a flat *pip*; song is burry *fee-BEEoh*.

WHERE TO FIND: WILLOW: Common migrant and summer resident (May-September) of riparian wetlands and willow thickets in southern part of region. Found at lower elevations in central part of region (e.g., Williams Lake). ALDER: Common migrant and summer resident in willow and alder thickets in the northern part of the region (plateaus north of Kamloops and Williams Lake). Probably migrates east out of region rather than south.

BEHAVIOUR: Both forage for insects and nest in willow and alder thickets.

DID YOU KNOW? Willow and Alder Flycatcher were once considered the same species—Traill's Flycatcher—but studies along the San Jose River between Lac La Hache and Williams Lake showed that they were instead two distinct—though very similar—species.

DATE AND LOCATION SEEN: ______________________

____

____

Pacific-slope/Cordilleran Flycatcher

Yellow-bellied Flycatcher

DESCRIPTION: 14 cm. These species are best identified by calls. YELLOW-BELLIED: **Upperparts are olive,** wings blackish with **white wing-bars**, breast olive-yellow, throat and belly usually distinctly yellowish. **Bold white eye-ring. Compact, short-tailed compared with other** *Empidonax* flycatchers. PACIFIC-SLOPE/CORDILLERAN: Virtually identical species, perhaps best considered as one. Very similar to Yellow-bellied, but longer tail, less contrast in wings, and **teardrop-shaped eye-ring** (pointed at rear).

SIMILAR SPECIES: Other *Empidonax* flycatchers lack the yellow throat, have different calls.

VOICE: YELLOW-BELLIED: Call is clear, rising *suwee*, song is *chelek*, similar to Least Flycatcher but lazier. PACIFIC-SLOPE/ CORDILLERAN: Call is up-slurred *suweet* (Pacific-slope) or *pee seet* (Cordilleran); song is three-parted *sileek, titik, seet.*

WHERE TO FIND: YELLOW-BELLIED: Uncommon and local in spruce bogs and replanted forests in north of region; rare in spruce forests on eastern Rockies (e.g., Kananaskis). PACIFIC-SLOPE/ CORDILLERAN: Locally common summer resident of shady creek valleys, especially with rocky bluffs; also lakeshores.

BEHAVIOUR: YELLOW-BELLIED: Grassy nest cup usually built on ground, embedded deep in moss or ferns. PACIFIC-SLOPE/ CORDILLERAN: Builds mossy nest on cliff ledges, roadcuts, under bridges, and under eaves of buildings.

DID YOU KNOW? Cordilleran and Pacific-slope Flycatchers were once considered a single species, the Western Flycatcher. Studies suggest much genetic intergradation between the two in the region.

DATE AND LOCATION SEEN: ______________________

____

____

Dusky Flycatcher

Gray Flycatcher

Dusky Flycatcher / Gray Flycatcher

Empidonax oberholseri / Empidonax wrighti

DESCRIPTION: 14.5 cm/15 cm. Small, slender flycatchers with greyish upperparts, **whitish or yellowish underparts**, **prominent whitish eye-rings**, dark grey wings with **prominent pale wing-bars**, and **long tails**. DUSKY: **dark bill pale at base**. GRAY: Long, narrow, **pale bill with a dark tip**.

SIMILAR SPECIES: Hammond's Flycatcher (p. 247) is more compact, with a shorter tail and very small, all-dark bill.

VOICE: Both species give dry *whit* calls. DUSKY: Song has three phrases, a high, fast *sibit*, a rough, nasal *tuwerp* and clear, high *sweet*; notes may be sung in any order. Soft *whit* call note, also a lazy *du-hic*. GRAY: Song is rough *chelep chelep, chelep sweep.*

WHERE TO FIND: DUSKY: Common migrant and summer resident (April–September) in dry, open coniferous and mixed forests with shrubby understories. GRAY: Rare and local in south Okanagan Valley in open ponderosa pine forests; Kilometre 10 of McKinney Road east of Oliver is a reliable location.

BEHAVIOUR: DUSKY: Forages for insects on or around trees and shrubs. Typically flies out from perches to catch insects on the wing. GRAY: Usually perches low and gleans insects above and around shrubs, often dropping down to the ground.

DID YOU KNOW? The Gray Flycatcher spread northward from California and Oregon in the 1970s and 1980s, reaching British Columbia in 1984.

DATE AND LOCATION SEEN: ______________________

____

____

Least Flycatcher

Hammond's Flycatcher

Least Flycatcher / Hammond's Flycatcher

Empidonax minimus / Empidonax hammondii

DESCRIPTION: 13 cm/14 cm. Small *Empidonax* flycatchers with proportionately large heads. LEAST: Olive-grey above, **pale below**. **Bold white eye-ring**, bill short and wide, **lower mandible mostly orange**. HAMMOND'S: **small**, **mostly dark and narrow bill**, relatively short tail, **olive-grey breast**, **greyish head**, and long wing tips. White eye-ring. The large head, tiny bill, and eye-ring give this small flycatcher a kinglet-like appearance.

SIMILAR SPECIES: Slimmer Dusky Flycatcher (p. 245) has longer tail, shorter wings.

VOICE: LEAST: Call a sharp *whit*; song a dry, constantly repeated *cheBEK, cheBEK, cheBEK*. HAMMOND'S: Call is high *peep*; song is three-part phrase *si-pik swivrk gra-vik.*

WHERE TO FIND: LEAST: Common to uncommon migrant and summer resident (May–September) throughout region, in deciduous woods, usually aspen copses. HAMMOND'S: Common migrant and summer resident (April–September) of coniferous forests with closed canopy. More widespread in migration.

BEHAVIOUR: LEAST: Aggressive and pugnacious, especially toward American Redstarts and Brown-headed Cowbirds. Territories are usually clustered. HAMMOND'S: Lifts tail forcefully upward, also flicks wings. Forages within canopy of shady forests, making quick sallies for insects.

DID YOU KNOW? Unlike the closely related Dusky Flycatcher, Hammond's undergoes its complete annual moult before it leaves its breeding grounds, and therefore migrates south later in autumn.

DATE AND LOCATION SEEN: ______________________

DESCRIPTION: 19 cm. Open-country flycatcher that is **greyish above** with a **salmon-coloured belly** and a **contrastingly blackish tail**. Juveniles have cinnamon wing-bars.

SIMILAR SPECIES: Larger Western Kingbird is yellow below and has white outer tail feathers.

VOICE: Call is rich, down-slurred whistle *pdeeer.* Song alternates between downslurred *pdeeew* and rising *pidireep.*

WHERE TO FIND: Common migrant and summer resident (February–September) of dry open country, rare in northern part of region; very rare in winter in south Okanagan.

BEHAVIOUR: Perches openly on fences, buildings, plant stems, boulders, and bare ground. Most foraging takes place at ground level. Often dips and spreads tail in a broad, shallow arc when perched. Nests wherever there is a sheltered ledge or cavity, usually on cliff faces, in trees, under rocks, or on building ledges.

DID YOU KNOW? Say's Phoebes are among the first migrants to arrive in spring, often when snow is still present.

DATE AND LOCATION SEEN: ______________________

____

____

Western Kingbird
Eastern Kingbird

DESCRIPTION: 22 cm/22 cm. WESTERN: Has **yellow belly. Pale grey upperparts**, head and breast; white throat provides little contrast. **Black tail has thin, white border along sides**. EASTERN: Dark grey above (darkest on head), **white below**, with **white tail tip**.

SIMILAR SPECIES: Say's Phoebe (p. 249) patterned like Western Kingbird, but is smaller, orange below, and has all-black tail.

VOICE: WESTERN: Calls include sharp *bik* and various sputtering notes; song is *pik pik peek PEEK-a-loo* crescendo. EASTERN: Call is buzzy *kzeeeer*; song is series of sharp, sputtering notes.

WHERE TO FIND: WESTERN: Common migrant and summer resident (April–August) in dry, open rangeland, agricultural areas, and open woodlands north to Quesnel. EASTERN: Common migrant and summer resident (mid-May–September) in open areas, gardens, orchards, and riparian woodlands, usually near water, rare at northern end of region.

BEHAVIOUR: Both species sally from high perches to catch insects; Westerns typically from utility poles or open grown shade trees and Easterns from streamside cottonwoods or willows. They also eat fruit. Both species build nests in trees, but Westerns also frequently nest on utility poles.

DID YOU KNOW? Both kingbirds are fearlessly aggressive in their defence of their nests, and will vociferously drive off or physically attack much larger birds that haplessly fly by.

DATE AND LOCATION SEEN: ______________________________

____

____

Adult

Immature

DESCRIPTION: 25 cm. Sleek, bull-headed, long-tailed predatory songbird with **bold black mask**; underparts pale; black wings and tail have white patches. Thick **black bill** has pale base to lower mandible and is **hooked at the tip**. Adult has pearl-grey head and back; **black mask** does not cross over base of lower bill. Juvenile like adult, with **buffy wash and distinct scaling on underparts**, faded plumage and paler bill, faint white eye-ring.

SIMILAR SPECIES: Any shrike seen in summer in the region is likely a Loggerhead Shrike (rare); has darker grey head and back, broad mask crosses over base of bill. Bill is short and stubby, lower mandible all black. Northern Mockingbird (rare) lacks black mask, has narrow, pointed bill.

VOICE: Call is nasal *fay fay*; occasionally heard singing a musical, warbling song.

WHERE TO FIND: Uncommon migrant and winter resident (September–April) in open areas.

BEHAVIOUR: Perches openly on fence lines, tops of shrubs, pouncing on prey (mice and small birds) with short flights. Flight is rapid and direct, often ending in a quick climb to perch.

DID YOU KNOW? Unlike raptors, shrikes lack powerful feet for grasping and dismembering prey, so they often impale prey on thorns or barbed wire to facilitate feeding, display for courtship, or to store for later use. This has earned them the nickname "butcher bird."

DATE AND LOCATION SEEN: ______________________

____

____

Cassin's Vireo
Vireo cassinii

DESCRIPTION: 14 cm. Stocky, short-tailed vireo with heavy bill, whitish underparts, **bold white spectacles**, and **whitish wing-bars**. Upperparts are **olive-grey**; has **pale yellow flanks** and grey head.

SIMILAR SPECIES: Red-eyed Vireo (p. 257) has a long, flat crown and a bold white eyebrow. Blue-headed Vireo (east of Rockies) has blue-grey crown and face that are sharply demarked from pure white throat and greenish back; also has bolder white wing-bars and more distinctive yellow flanks. Warbling Vireo (p. 257) lacks white wing-bars and spectacles.

VOICE: Burry, whistled song with notes inflected upward and downward. Harsh scolding calls.

WHERE TO FIND: Common migrant and summer resident (April–October) of open coniferous or mixed forests.

BEHAVIOUR: Gleans insects slowly and deliberately in upper tree canopy. Persistent singer, often heard throughout the day during the breeding season.

DID YOU KNOW? The Cassin's Vireo was once considered conspecific with the eastern-dwelling Blue-headed Vireo and southwestern Plumbeous Vireo; all three were known collectively as the Solitary Vireo.

DATE AND LOCATION SEEN: ______________________

____

____

Warbling Vireo
Red-eyed Vireo

Warbling Vireo / Red-eyed Vireo

Vireo gilvus / Vireo olivaceus

DESCRIPTION: 14 cm/15 cm. These vireos **lack wing-bars**. WARBLING: **Plain brownish-olive above**, whitish below, with **distinct pale eyebrow**. RED-EYED: Has **uniform olive-green upperparts**, white and pale yellow below. **Long**, **flat grey crown** sharply borders **conspicuous white eyebrow**; **dark eye-line** runs through **red eye**; has long, heavy bill.

SIMILAR SPECIES: Cassin's Vireo (p. 255) has white spectacles and wing-bars.

VOICE: WARBLING: Call is harsh, nasal *reeish*; song is rapid warble of high and low notes accented at the end. RED-EYED: Calls include soft, nasal *reer* or descending *myaah*; song is a series of rising and falling whistled phrases with brief pause between each phrase, like questions and answers.

WHERE TO FIND: WARBLING: Common migrant and summer resident (April–September) of riparian areas, aspen copses, and young shrubby forests. RED-EYED: Uncommon to common migrant and summer resident (late May–September) of deciduous riparian woodlands, especially cottonwoods.

BEHAVIOUR: Both glean insects slowly and deliberately in upper tree canopy. Persistent singers, they can often be heard throughout the day even on the hottest July days when other songbirds are silent.

DID YOU KNOW? Timber harvest and fire open up coniferous forest canopies, creating shrubby habitats that favour Warbling Vireos.

DATE AND LOCATION SEEN: ______________________

____

____

Adult

Juvenile

DESCRIPTION: 29 cm. ADULT: Has **dark grey upperparts**, **light grey underparts**, and **dark crown**; **face, neck, and forehead are white**. Bill is dark, short, and stout. IMMATURE: Dark sooty grey with whitish moustache stripe.

SIMILAR SPECIES: Clark's Nutcracker (p. 263) has black wings with prominent white patches, a shorter, black and white tail, and long bill.

VOICE: Call is short series of soft, whistled notes, commonly a clear *wheeoo.*

WHERE TO FIND: Uncommon resident of mid- to high-elevation boreal and subalpine coniferous forests.

BEHAVIOUR: Mainly forages from perches, flying from tree to tree in search of various foods, including insects, fruit, small vertebrates, and carrion. Gregarious, often travelling through the forest in family groups. Sometimes makes altitudinal migrations to lower elevation areas in late fall and winter.

DID YOU KNOW? Gray Jays are also called Canada jays or whisky jacks.

DATE AND LOCATION SEEN: ______________________

____

____

Steller's Jay
Blue Jay

DESCRIPTION: 29 cm/28 cm. STELLER'S: **Blackish crested head** shows white eye crescents, forehead marks, and streaks on throat. Back is charcoal grey; all **other plumage cobalt blue**. Wings and tail show fine black barring. BLUE: **Pale blue upperparts and greyish-white underparts**. Has white wing markings and tail corners, fine black bands on wings and tail. **Head has distinctive blue crest**; **pale throat** outlined by **black necklace**.

SIMILAR SPECIES: Nothing similar in region.

VOICE: STELLER'S: Call is harsh *shek shek shek*. Other calls include imitation of Red-tailed Hawk scream. BLUE: Common call is nasal *jaaaay*.

WHERE TO FIND: STELLER'S: Common resident of coniferous and mixed forests and residential areas with mature trees. BLUE: Uncommon resident of deciduous or mixed park-like forests, often residential areas, in East Kootenay region of British Columbia and eastern slopes of Rockies. Rare and irregular fall migrant and winter resident (October–February) elsewhere.

BEHAVIOUR: Both omnivorous. Forage for seeds, fruits, insects, and other invertebrates; also feed on small vertebrates, other birds' eggs and nestlings. Steller's commonly moves downslope in fall to low-elevation valleys in search of food; mixed feeding flocks of these two species readily visit bird feeders. Both are very vocal outside of the breeding season, quiet and secretive around breeding territories.

DID YOU KNOW? The Steller's Jay is the official provincial bird of British Columbia.

DATE AND LOCATION SEEN: ______________________

____

____

Clark's Nutcracker
Nucifraga columbiana

DESCRIPTION: 30 cm. Large and **grey** all over with a **white patch on black wings**; has broad white borders to a short black tail. Undertail is white. Has a long, pointed black bill.

SIMILAR SPECIES: Gray Jay (p. 259) lacks black wings and tail, has shorter bill and longer tail.

VOICE: A long harsh *kraaaaaaaa*.

WHERE TO FIND: Fairly common resident of coniferous forests, rare and local on north-central plateaus. Wanders widely in years when pine seed crops are poor. Common and conspicuous in mountain parks in Rockies, Manning Park in Cascades.

BEHAVIOUR: Mainly feeds on seeds of ponderosa and whitebark pines. Begins nesting in late winter, relying on pine seed caches for food supply. At times, wanders extensively in search of food, sometimes in large flocks.

DID YOU KNOW? Clark's Nutcracker has an incredible spatial memory, enabling it to find in winter most of the tens of thousands of seeds cached in the late summer and fall.

DATE AND LOCATION SEEN: ______________________

____

____

DESCRIPTION: 48 cm. Fairly large corvid with **black head, upper-parts**, and undertail area. **White flanks, shoulder patch, and belly**; and **iridescent green wings and tail**. **Tail is long and wedge-shaped**. In flight, **broad white wing patch** is prominent.

SIMILAR SPECIES: Differentiated from other jays and Clark's Nutcracker (p. 263) by combination of black upperparts, white belly, and long tail.

VOICE: Calls include a rising *jeeeek* and rapid *shek shek shek.*

WHERE TO FIND: Common resident of rangelands, farms, and other open country, especially riparian areas with scattered deciduous trees and shrubs. Many migrate south from northern part of region.

BEHAVIOUR: Omnivorous. Feeds mostly on insects in summer and wide variety of foods including seeds, berries, small vertebrates, and carrion in other seasons. Builds large stick nests with domed canopies in shrubs or trees, and forages in a variety of open habitats, including agricultural and residential areas. Forms large, noisy roosts in winter, sometimes numbering several hundred birds. Like other corvids, magpies are gregarious, vocal, and intelligent.

DID YOU KNOW? Many bird species use abandoned old magpie nests for their nests and roost sites, including Merlins and Long-eared Owls.

DATE AND LOCATION SEEN: ______________________

____

____

DESCRIPTION: 45 cm, wingspan 99 cm. Familiar large, chunky, **all-black** bird with a **heavy black bill**, **and square or slightly rounded tail**.

SIMILAR SPECIES: Common Raven (p. 269) has longer, more pointed wings, longer wedge-shaped tail, heavier bill, and shaggy throat feathers, different calls.

VOICE: Call is repeated *caw caw caw*.

WHERE TO FIND: Common widespread resident of low-elevation open valleys, most often around agricultural and residential areas with trees. Concentrations occur in valleys with open water and abundant food resources in winter.

BEHAVIOUR: Intelligent and inquisitive omnivores that forage in many ways, including scavenging dead animals, availing themselves of abundant seed crops or insects, preying upon small vertebrates, or gleaning through trash. Bold and abundant, they are usually wary of people. Gather into large winter flocks to feed and roost.

DID YOU KNOW? The American Crow is very closely related to its smaller, coastal cousin, the Northwestern Crow. The two species are so similar that even expert birders disagree where the geographical boundary between the two species lies, but all would agree that the birds east of the Coast and Cascade mountains are American Crows.

DATE AND LOCATION SEEN: ______________________

____

____

DESCRIPTION: 61 cm, wingspan 117 cm. Region's largest songbird, being almost half again the length and twice the weight of the American Crow. **All black**, with long pointed wings, **wedge-shaped tail**, **very heavy black bill**, and thin, lance-like feathers on the throat.

SIMILAR SPECIES: Smaller American Crow (p. 267) has square or slightly rounded tail, and much different voice.

VOICE: Common calls are deep, resonant croaks. Also gives hollow knocking calls and higher gurgling notes.

WHERE TO FIND: Common widespread resident throughout region. Large numbers gather at most landfills.

BEHAVIOUR: Unlike crows, ravens routinely soar high in the air like hawks. Omnivorous, they often feed on roadkills along highways, refuse at landfills and dumpsters. Effective predators, they also take rodents, reptiles, and eggs and young of many bird species. Build large stick nests, usually on cliff faces or in large trees.

DID YOU KNOW? Bold and resourceful, ravens are considered among the most intelligent of all birds.

DATE AND LOCATION SEEN: ______________________

____

____

DESCRIPTION: 18 cm. Flocking songbird of open country. Pinkish-brown above, mostly white below. **Tail is black with brown centre and white edges**. MALE: Has **black bib** on breast, black cheek patch, black bar across forecrown with small projecting feathers ("horns"). **Throat and eyebrow yellow or white**. FEMALE: Duller with less contrasting pattern. JUVENILE: Streaked and spotted, suggesting a sparrow or pipit.

SIMILAR SPECIES: American Pipit (p. 329) is darker, more slender, and streaked on breast. Lapland Longspur (p. 385) has thicker bill and is heavily streaked and barred above.

VOICE: Flight calls include *tseep*, *tew*, and *zip* notes. Song starts with *terp* notes, followed by rising, tinkling flourish; often given in high, sustained flight.

WHERE TO FIND: Uncommon to fairly common migrant and summer resident, rare winter resident in sparsely vegetated, open areas. Two subspecies breed in region, a white-faced race in alpine tundra and a yellow-faced race in dry grasslands in Nicola and Thompson valleys and Chilcotin Plateau.

BEHAVIOUR: A ground bird, but will perch on low shrubs and fence lines. Found in pairs in the breeding season, but in fall and winter gathers into large flocks that wheel about low over open fields.

DID YOU KNOW? Horned Larks perform elaborate breeding displays. A male flies up high into the sky, sings his high, tinkling songs above a prospective mate as he circles her ground position, then folds his wings and plunges to the ground.

DATE AND LOCATION SEEN: ____________________

____

____

DESCRIPTION: 14.5 cm. Bicoloured swallow, **entirely dark above** (including through the eyes) and **white below**. **Tail is slightly forked**. MALE: Deep **iridescent steel blue** to blue-green above, pure white below. FEMALE: Variable; usually much duller above than male, with slate-brown cast. JUVENILE: Brown above, variable tinge of grey across the breast.

SIMILAR SPECIES: Smaller Violet-green Swallow (p. 275) is shorter-tailed, has white around the eyes, and white patches on the sides of rump. Bank Swallow (p. 279) resembles juvenile Tree but has distinct brown breast band, pale brown rump, and pale area behind cheeks. Northern Rough-winged Swallow (p. 277) resembles juvenile Tree, but has a brown throat.

VOICE: Calls have rich, liquid quality: *treep* or *chirp*; song is series of liquid chirps and whistles.

WHERE TO FIND: Common migrant (late February–May, July–October) and summer resident, usually concentrated around wetlands, rivers, and lakes, but also on open grasslands.

BEHAVIOUR: Like all swallows, spends most of the day on the wing foraging for flying insects. Perches on wires, bare limbs, and bulrushes; usually over water. Nests in cavities of trees; uses nest boxes placed near water or in open grasslands.

DID YOU KNOW? Hardy Tree Swallows winter farther north than any other American swallows, and are one of the earliest to arrive in region in spring.

DATE AND LOCATION SEEN: ______________________

____

____

Violet-green Swallow

Tachycineta thalassina

DESCRIPTION: 13 cm. Small, **short-tailed**, **green-backed** swallow with white underparts, **white on the face over the eye**, and **white sides to the rump**. MALE: Has bright emerald-green back and crown, purple rump. FEMALE: Has duller back and rump; face pattern is more obscure.

SIMILAR SPECIES: Tree Swallow (p. 273) has white underparts, but lacks white over the eye and white rump patches; shows a deep bluish-green back.

VOICE: Most common call is sharp, *chilp* or *chip-lip*; song is rhythmic series of *chip*, *tseep*, and *chew* notes.

WHERE TO FIND: Common migrant (April–May, August–September) and summer resident of rocky cliffs, canyons, and residential areas; often gathers in large foraging flocks over lakes and rivers.

BEHAVIOUR: Nests colonially on cliff face crevices (often with White-throated Swifts), also singly in tree cavities, on buildings and other man-made structures, and in nest boxes.

DID YOU KNOW? In summer, Violet-green Swallows can be active and very vocal well before dawn.

DATE AND LOCATION SEEN: ______________________

____

____

Northern Rough-winged Swallow

Stelgidopteryx serripennis

DESCRIPTION: 14 cm. **Dull brownish head and upperparts**, dingy white underparts with a **diffuse, pale brownish wash on throat, breast, and sides**. Tail is squared or very slightly notched; wings are long. JUVENILE: Resembles adult but with cinnamon wing-bars.

SIMILAR SPECIES: Similar juvenile Tree Swallow (p. 273) has a white throat. Smaller Bank Swallow (p. 279) is shorter winged, has a paler back, and a distinct breast band contrasting with its white throat.

VOICE: Call is low, coarse *prriit.*

WHERE TO FIND: Fairly common migrant and summer resident (April–September) along rivers, lakes, and marshes at low- to mid-elevations.

BEHAVIOUR: Flight is buoyant, with swept-back wingbeats. Often forages over water but also over open fields and meadows. Nests in holes in earthen banks, but also uses artificial sites under bridges or other structures. Does not nest colonially.

DID YOU KNOW? The Rough-winged Swallow gets its name from small serrations on the outer edge of its outermost flight feathers. The function of these serrations remains unknown.

DATE AND LOCATION SEEN: ____________________

DESCRIPTION: 13 cm. North America's **smallest swallow**. Head and back are greyish-brown, wings and tail darker. **Underparts, including throat and cheek, are white** with **distinct brown breast band**.

SIMILAR SPECIES: Northern Rough-winged Swallow (p. 277) has dingy grey throat and breast, lacks distinct breast band. Juvenile Tree Swallow (p. 273) has incomplete pale grey breast band.

VOICE: Call is dry, harsh *churr*, usually repeated rapidly.

WHERE TO FIND: Common migrant (April–May, July–September) and locally common summer resident of open, lowland areas in valleys.

BEHAVIOUR: Forages on the wing for flying insects, usually in flocks flying over ponds, lakes, and rivers. Diagnostic flight is fast, with fluttery, shallow wingbeats. Nests colonially in vertical silt bluffs, streamside banks or gravel pit walls. In late summer, birds gather into large flocks prior to migration.

DID YOU KNOW? The Bank Swallow is one of the most widely distributed swallows in the world; in Europe it is known as the Sand Martin.

DATE AND LOCATION SEEN: ____________________

DESCRIPTION: 14 cm. **Square-tailed** swallow with **chestnut throat and cheek that contrasts with white underparts**. **White forehead** contrasts with dark cap; upperparts with white back streaking and distinct **buff rump patch**. Wings broader and relatively shorter than Tree or Barn Swallows. JUVENILE: Duller and less strongly patterned, with variable white spotting in dull blackish-brown throat.

SIMILAR SPECIES: Barn Swallow (p. 283) has dark forehead, strongly forked tail, dark rump.

VOICE: Calls include rough *vrrrt* or *veer* notes, a more musical *veeew*, and a prolonged song of grating, creaking notes.

WHERE TO FIND: Common migrant and summer resident (April–September) in open areas. Large colonies occur on cliffs along lakes, under bridges, and on large buildings in suitable habitat.

BEHAVIOUR: Often seen in large flocks. Typical flight includes circling and steep upward climbs. Builds a distinctive gourd-shaped nest from mud pellets, usually located under protective ledge or roof.

DID YOU KNOW? Gray-crowned Rosy-Finches frequently roost in abandoned Cliff Swallow nests in winter.

DATE AND LOCATION SEEN: ______________________________

____

____

DESCRIPTION: 17 cm. Large, slender swallow with a **very long, deeply forked tail**. MALE: Deep steel-blue above, with a **chestnut forehead and throat**, **orangish underparts**. White spots show on spread tail. FEMALE: Resembles male, but tail is shorter; underparts are paler. JUVENILE: Has even shorter, but still strongly forked tail; underparts are whitish-buff.

SIMILAR SPECIES: Shorter-tailed juveniles can suggest Cliff Swallow (p. 281), but have dark rump and prominent tail notch.

VOICE: Call is scratchy *vit* or *vit-WHEET*; song combines *vit* calls with other scratchy notes.

WHERE TO FIND: Common migrant (March–April, August–October) and summer resident, uncommon at higher elevations and in urban areas.

BEHAVIOUR: Forages on the wing for flying insects; usually flies low over open fields or water. Nests almost exclusively on human structures such as bridges, barns, and other structures with vertical or horizontal walls or beams that are under cover. Does not form dense colonies, though several pairs often nest in the same structure. Flocks of thousands gather in late summer prior to migration.

DID YOU KNOW? Barn Swallow populations have been declining steadily for the past 30 years.

DATE AND LOCATION SEEN: ______________________________

____

____

Black-capped Chickadee

Mountain Chickadee

Black-capped Chickadee / Mountain Chickadee

Poecile atricapillus / Poecile gambeli

DESCRIPTION: 13 cm/12 cm. BLACK-CAPPED: Small. **White cheek patch separates black head and throat**. Tiny, dark bill, grey back, pale grey or buff flanks, white underparts. MOUNTAIN: Has grey upperparts, greyish-white lowerparts, **black crown and throat**, and bold **white eyebrow**.

SIMILAR SPECIES: Boreal and Chestnut-backed Chickadees (p. 287) have brownish sides and greyer caps, more nasal calls.

VOICE: BLACK-CAPPED: Call is clear *chick a dee dee dee*; song is high, whistled *fee-bee* or *fee-bee-bee*, with second and third notes lower than first. MOUNTAIN: Call is harsh *shika zee zee*; song is whistled *see see bee bee*, with second note lower than first but higher than third and fourth.

WHERE TO FIND: BLACK-CAPPED: Common resident of riparian woodlands, deciduous or mixed forests, and residential areas. MOUNTAIN: Common resident of coniferous forests; uncommon to rare at northern edge of region.

BEHAVIOUR: Both species forage for insects by gleaning, hovering, and probing vegetation. Also feed on seeds and readily accept suet and birdseed at feeders. They nest in tree cavities, occasionally in nest boxes. Form foraging flocks outside of the breeding season, often with other species. Often mob predatory birds.

DID YOU KNOW? The number of *dee dee dee* notes at the end of the Black-capped Chickadee's call increases when a predator is nearby.

DATE AND LOCATION SEEN: ______________________

____

____

Boreal Chickadee
Chestnut-backed Chickadee

DESCRIPTION: 14 cm/12 cm. Small, acrobatic, and unwary birds of coniferous forests that have dark crowns and throats with **contrasting white cheek patches**, greyish wings. BOREAL: Has brownish grey upperparts, **brownish crown** and black throat, and **buffy brown sides**. CHESTNUT-BACKED: Smaller, shorter-tailed. Has **blackish-brown crown and throat**, rich **chestnut back and flanks**.

SIMILAR SPECIES: Black-capped Chickadee (p. 285) has black cap, grey back, pale buff sides; Mountain Chickadee (p. 285) has white eyebrow.

VOICE: BOREAL: Call is harsh *tsi-si-jay-jay*. CHESTNUT-BACKED: Calls include high, buzzy *zee dee* notes, nasal *shik-a-jee-jee*.

WHERE TO FIND: BOREAL: Common resident of upper subalpine forests. CHESTNUT-BACKED: Common resident of moist coniferous forests (hemlock-red cedar), mostly in Columbia Mountains and on west slope of Rocky Mountains.

BEHAVIOUR: Both species forage, often acrobatically, by gleaning insects from the surfaces of leaves and needles. They use tree cavities for nesting and excitedly mob predatory birds. Chestnut-backed Chickadees occasionally move into drier forests and residential areas in fall and winter, Boreal Chickadees rarely move down from their mountaintop habitats.

DID YOU KNOW? Both species cache food items, including birdseed, for later retrieval and consumption.

DATE AND LOCATION SEEN: ______________________

____

____

DESCRIPTION: 11.5 cm. Region's only nuthatch with a **black line through the eye and a white eyebrow**. Crown is black (male) or grey (female), upperparts are grey, and **underparts are orange cinnamon** (paler in female).

SIMILAR SPECIES: Larger White-breasted Nuthatch (p. 291) has white underparts and face, and a rust-coloured undertail. Smaller Pygmy Nuthatch (p. 293) lacks the white eyebrow.

VOICE: Call is a nasal *yank yank yank*.

WHERE TO FIND: Common resident of coniferous forests, but numbers are highly variable; dependent upon available food supply. Uncommon and irregular migrant and winter resident of low-elevation valleys.

BEHAVIOUR: Feeds on insects, spiders, and conifer seeds in forests, and birdseed or suet at bird feeders. Nests in cavities in snags and branches. Acrobatic: probes crevices in tree bark and climbs down tree trunks head first. Stores food for later use under bark, in holes, and in the ground.

DID YOU KNOW? Red-breasted Nuthatches often smear pitch around the entrance to their nest cavities to deter predators.

DATE AND LOCATION SEEN: ______________________________

____

____

DESCRIPTION: 14.5 cm. Small, stubby-tailed grey and white climbing bird with a **dark crown.** Has a **white face** and underparts; **rufous area under tail**. **Bill is long**, **slender**, **and chisel-like**. Grey and black tail shows white patches near the corners. MALE: Has black crown and hindneck. FEMALE: Crown and hindneck are dark grey.

SIMILAR SPECIES: Red-breasted Nuthatch (p. 289) has rusty underparts, white eyeline. Pygmy Nuthatch (p. 293) is smaller, lacks black crown and white face.

VOICE: Common call is nasal, trilled whinny *tidi-tidi-tidi.* Birds in northern end of region have very different call, a nasal, descending *renk*.

WHERE TO FIND: Uncommon to fairly common year-round resident in open ponderosa pine forests north to Thompson Valley; rare but increasing in residential areas in northern part of region, mainly in winter. Most easily found in south Okanagan Valley and southern Rocky Mountain Trench.

BEHAVIOUR: Acrobatic, creeping head-first down trunks and branches. Hammers at bark and seeds with wedge-tipped bill. Often seen in pairs or small family groups. Nests in cavities in snags or live trees, sometimes using abandoned woodpecker nest holes or nest boxes.

DID YOU KNOW? The White-breasted Nuthatch has three subspecies that have different vocalizations and may represent distinct species.

DATE AND LOCATION SEEN: ______________________

____

____

DESCRIPTION: 11 cm. Excitable, active twittering nuthatch that feeds high in ponderosa pines. **Tiny**, with **greyish upperparts**, **buffy-white underparts** and greyish flanks. **Greyish-brown crown** is bordered by dark eye-line, whitish face and throat. Bill is relatively long and tail is short.

SIMILAR SPECIES: Larger White-breasted Nuthatch (p. 291) has a bright white face, rusty undertail. Larger Red-breasted Nuthatch (p. 289) has a distinct white eyebrow.

VOICE: Call is high, rapid twittering *pip-pip-pip* notes, often given in chorus by a flock; also gives high chipping, squeaky notes.

WHERE TO FIND: Fairly common resident of dry, open mature ponderosa pine forests with snags. Somewhat more widespread in winter, but seldom far from ponderosa pines. Most common in the Okanagan Valley, but also found in the Similkameen, Thompson, and Nicola valleys; rare in the East Kootenay Valley.

BEHAVIOUR: Usually seen in flocks. Acrobatically forages for insects or pine seeds high in ponderosa pine branches. Gleans from foliage, probes bark crevices and cones, and scales off loose bark. Gregarious except when nesting, and often joins multi-species feeding flocks. Roosts and nests in tree cavities. Caches seeds.

DID YOU KNOW? In winter, Pygmy Nuthatches roost communally in tree cavities; some large holes are home to more than a hundred birds overnight.

DATE AND LOCATION SEEN: ______________________

____

____

DESCRIPTION: 13 cm. **Tiny**, cryptic **trunk-creeping bird** with a long, thin **down-curved bill**. **Mottled brownish-grey** above with whitish eyebrow, long buffy wing-stripe, and rusty rump; whitish below. Has long, stiff tail.

SIMILAR SPECIES: Nuthatches lack mottled-brown upperparts and down-curved bill.

VOICE: Best recognized by very high, thin *tseeee* note; song is rhythmic *see-seee, seedly-see.*

WHERE TO FIND: Fairly common resident of mature coniferous and mixed forests. More widespread in winter. Some migratory movements noted (April–May, October–November).

BEHAVIOUR: Forages for insects picked from tree bark crevices. Feeds by flying to the base of a tree and creeping upward, spiralling around the trunk until it reaches the top. Then it flies to the next tree and repeats the process. Builds nest under loose sections of tree bark. Frequently encountered in mixed species foraging flocks outside of the breeding season.

DID YOU KNOW? The mottled plumage of Brown Creepers strongly resembles conifer tree bark. When the bird senses danger it stops moving and relies upon its camouflaged coloration to help avoid detection.

DATE AND LOCATION SEEN: ______________________________

____

____

Rock Wren
Canyon Wren

DESCRIPTION: 15 cm/14.5 cm. ROCK WREN: **Pale grey-brown** with **buff belly**. Back speckled with white; whitish **breast** is **finely streaked**; head has whitish eyebrow; tail is barred; bill is long, thin. CANYON WREN: Dark **rufous-brown back** with pale and dark spots; **rufous breast** with faint dark bars; **tail bright rufous** with thin, black barring; head pale and dark-spotted grey; **throat contrasting white**. **Bill very long**, thin, slightly decurved.

SIMILAR SPECIES: Bewick's Wren (rare in Okanagan Valley) has conspicuous white eyebrow. House Wren (p. 299) is brown, barred with black.

VOICE: ROCK WREN: Call is trilled *pidzeee* and *deee-dee*; song has buzzy, repeated, trilled phrases. CANYON WREN: Call is loud buzzy *jeep*; unmistakable song is loud cascading series of clear whistles, falling and slowing down.

WHERE TO FIND: ROCK WREN: Common summer resident in southern valleys (April–October), rare in winter. Found at sunny rock outcroppings, rockslides, and rocky fields. CANYON WREN: Fairly common resident of rocky cliffs in south Okanagan and lower Similkameen, rare and local in West Kootenay.

BEHAVIOUR: Both forage for insects and spiders almost exclusively on rocks, talus slopes. ROCK WREN: Prefers open, sunny areas, including rocky deserts. CANYON WREN: Favours cracks and crevices, with vertical rock walls or outcrops. Both build nests deep within rock crevices.

DID YOU KNOW? Rock Wrens often place many small pebbles at the entrance to their nest cavities. Their function is unknown.

DATE AND LOCATION SEEN: ______________________

____

____

DESCRIPTION: 12 cm. **Plain brownish** with **fine black barring** on wings, flanks, undertail, tail. Has thin, indistinct eyebrow.

SIMILAR SPECIES: Smaller Winter Wren (p. 301) is all dark brown with short tail. Marsh Wren (p. 303) has striped back, shorter tail, with rusty wings and rump. Bewick's Wren (very rare) has clear grey breast and distinct white eyebrow.

VOICE: Extremely varied. Common calls include musical *jirrd* or mewing notes. Bubbly song consists of series of rattles and trills.

WHERE TO FIND: Common migrant and summer resident (April–September) of riparian areas, open woodlands, and residential areas with open space and trees; rare north of the Thompson Valley.

BEHAVIOUR: Gleans insects from foliage in brushy areas. Nests in natural cavities, woodpecker nest holes, or constructed nest boxes.

DID YOU KNOW? House Wrens will destroy the eggs of other wrens or songbirds nesting nearby.

DATE AND LOCATION SEEN: ________________________

DESCRIPTION: 10 cm. **Tiny**, shy waif of dark, brushy habitats. **Dark brown all over** with rufous-brown breast. Fine black barring on wings, flanks, and tail. **Short tail is usually cocked upward**. Has thin, indistinct buffy eyebrow.

SIMILAR SPECIES: Larger House Wren (p. 299) has paler underparts and longer tail.

VOICE: Call is emphatic *chip-chip*; song is a long and complex series of high, thin tinkling trills.

WHERE TO FIND: Fairly common summer resident (May–September) of dense, moist coniferous forests, often riparian areas. Moves south and downslope in winter to low-elevation brushy riparian woodlands in southern valleys.

BEHAVIOUR: Actively and methodically forages for insects and other invertebrates on the ground; typically in low shrubs, around logs, through brush piles, or under stream banks. Nests often built in natural cavities, usually in dead trees on or near the ground; also in mossy vertical banks. Male sometimes builds numerous nests.

DID YOU KNOW? The Winter Wren is probably best considered two species. Birds found east of the Rockies are genetically distinct from those west of the Rockies. The eastern birds sing slower, shorter, more musical songs than western birds, and both types tend to mate only with their own kind.

DATE AND LOCATION SEEN: ______________________________

____

____

Marsh Wren

Cistothorus palustris

DESCRIPTION: 13 cm. Small, busy marsh denizen with dark crown, **whitish eyebrow**, **black-and-white striped back**, **rusty wings and rump**. Has a dull whitish breast with tan flanks and belly. **Short tail is held vertically**. Long, thin bill curves down. JUVENILE: Patterning more subdued than adult's.

SIMILAR SPECIES: Larger Bewick's Wren (very rare) has bolder white eyebrow, plain back. House Wren (p. 299) is uniform, plain brown with only a very faint eyebrow.

VOICE: Call is hard *tek*; song is gurgling, rattling trill that begins with a few call notes.

WHERE TO FIND: Common migrant (April–May, September–October) and summer resident of bulrush marshes, rare to uncommon at northern end of region. Uncommon and local in winter in cattail marshes in southern valleys.

BEHAVIOUR: Gleans for insects beneath dense bulrush cover. Often stays well hidden, but singing birds often sit more openly. Male sings day or night. Nest is a woven football-like structure attached to reeds.

DID YOU KNOW? A male Marsh Wren builds multiple nests for the female, and then she selects the one she finds most suitable. The chosen nest is then lined with bulrush down before the eggs are laid.

DATE AND LOCATION SEEN: ______________________

____

____

DESCRIPTION: 19 cm. **Chunky**, **slate-grey** streamside bird with a **short tail**, thin, dark bill, and long legs. Frequently flashes white eyelids and **bobs** up and down.

SIMILAR SPECIES: Distinctive species; larger and darker than wrens.

VOICE: Call is high, buzzy *dzeet*; song is series of high whistled or trilled phrases.

WHERE TO FIND: Fairly common resident of clear, fast mountain streams with cascades, riffles, and waterfalls. In late fall many move downstream to winter along lower-elevation streams and rivers. Regularly seen along Bow, Crooked, Nautley, Nechako, Okanagan (at weirs), Seton, and Similkameen rivers.

BEHAVIOUR: Mainly forages for aquatic insects. Flies rapidly up and down streams, actively patrols for food or defends territory. Bobs on emergent rocks; swims, dives, or wades through the water, and often disappears for short periods below the surface. When underwater, strides along stream bottoms by rowing with powerful wings. Builds domed nest from moss along streamsides or under bridges.

DID YOU KNOW? Compared to other songbirds, dippers have an extra thick coat of feathers, a lower metabolism and higher capacity to carry oxygen in their blood, all adaptations for life in and under very cold water. They cannot survive temperatures above 36°C, one of the reasons they nest in moist, shady situations.

DATE AND LOCATION SEEN: ______________________

____

____

Golden-crowned Kinglet

Ruby-crowned Kinglet

Regulus satrapa / Regulus calendula

DESCRIPTION: 10 cm/11 cm. GOLDEN-CROWNED: **Tiny**, with olive-grey upperparts, greyish-white underparts, dark flight feathers with golden edging and **white wing-bars**. Tail is short and notched, bill is tiny and thin. Has broad **white eyebrow below black crown stripe**. Crown centre is orange in male, golden-yellow in female. RUBY-CROWNED: Similar to Golden-crowned, but **olive overall with broken white eye-ring**. Male's bright red crest usually hidden unless bird is agitated. **Both species nervously flick wings**.

SIMILAR SPECIES: Warblers are larger than kinglets, and do not flick wings. Vireos are larger, more robust.

VOICE: GOLDEN-CROWNED: Call is high, thin *tsee*. Song starts with high, thin notes, ends in tumbling series. RUBY-CROWNED: Call is husky, dry *chi-dit*. Song starts with high, thin descending notes that build into loud and warbled, repeated phrases.

WHERE TO FIND: GOLDEN-CROWNED: Common resident of moister low- to mid-elevation coniferous forests; partial migrant, very rare in winter in northern parts of region. RUBY-CROWNED: Abundant migrant throughout region (April–May, September–October), common summer resident of subalpine and northern coniferous forests, rare in winter in southern valleys.

BEHAVIOUR: Both species forage and nest in coniferous trees, feed by gleaning insects from tree and shrub branches. Gregarious, form post-breeding flocks.

DID YOU KNOW? After the breeding season, kinglets, chickadees, and other species typically form flocks that forage together through tree and shrub canopies in search of food.

DATE AND LOCATION SEEN: ______________________

____

____

Western Bluebird
Male
Western Bluebird
Female
Mountain Bluebird
Male
Mountain Bluebird
Female

Western Bluebird / Mountain Bluebird

Sialia mexicana / Sialia currucoides

DESCRIPTION: 18 cm. WESTERN: Small, plump thrush with a short tail and long pointed wings. **Indigo blue head**, **wings**, **rump**, and **tail**. **Breast**, **sides**, **and variable patch on back are rusty brown.** Female's plumage is greyer, paler, but always has some rusty colour on breast. MOUNTAIN: Slimmer, longer-tailed, and longer-winged than Western. Male is **brilliant sky blue**, with whitish belly and undertail. Female is light grey overall, with blue wings and tail. Juveniles of both species like females but browner, heavily spotted.

SIMILAR SPECIES: Male Lazuli Bunting (p. 389) similar to male Western, but has bold white wing-bars, finch-like bill.

VOICE: WESTERN: Call is musical *tew*. MOUNTAIN: Call is lower, softer *phew*. Also has sharper alarm call: *tack*.

WHERE TO FIND: WESTERN: Fairly common migrant (February–April, September–November) and summer resident of open ponderosa pine forests and low-elevation forest edges north to Thompson Valley. Locally common in winter in south Okanagan around Russian olives and vineyards. MOUNTAIN: Common migrant (February–March, September–October) and summer resident in open areas ranging from valley grasslands to alpine meadows.

BEHAVIOUR: Both species capture insects using a variety of techniques; also feed on berries, especially in winter. Both nest in natural cavities in trees, woodpecker holes, and nest boxes.

DID YOU KNOW? Bluebird populations have benefited greatly from the installation of nest boxes, mostly because of limited available nesting cavities and competition from other cavity-nesters, especially European Starlings.

DATE AND LOCATION SEEN: ______________________________

____

____

DESCRIPTION: 22 cm. Slim, dull-coloured thrush. **Long-tailed** and short-billed. **Plain grey** all over with bold **white eye-ring**; buffy wing patch and **white tail sides** show in flight. Juveniles have scaly plumage.

SIMILAR SPECIES: Northern Mockingbird (rare) lacks white eye-ring, has distinct white wing-bars and wing patches. Smaller female Mountain Bluebird (p. 309) has a much shorter tail, blue in wings and tail, and lacks buffy wing patch.

VOICE: Call is distinctive soft, piping *peeh*; song is long, finch-like warble, often given in flight.

WHERE TO FIND: Fairly common summer resident of open coniferous forests. Common migrant and winter resident (October–April) at lower elevations in southern valleys, primarily in residential gardens or open woodlands with junipers.

BEHAVIOUR: Forages mainly for insects, other invertebrates, and berries in summer; feeds almost exclusively on berries in winter. Flycatches and also gleans insects from foliage on the ground. Nests on or near the ground in cavities with overhanging cover, often in cutbanks along roads.

DID YOU KNOW? Townsend's Solitaires defend their winter territories aggressively from other berry-eating birds.

DATE AND LOCATION SEEN: ____________________

____

____

DESCRIPTION: 18 cm. Medium-sized thrush of low-elevation riparian areas. **Upperparts** are **reddish-brown**; **breast is buffy with indistinct brown spots**, and belly is greyish.

SIMILAR SPECIES: Swainson's (p. 315) and Hermit Thrushes (p. 317) have prominent spotting on their breasts and grey- or olive-brown backs.

VOICE: Call is nasal *veer*; song is flutelike, descending *vree, vee-ur, vee-ur, veer, veer, veer, veer.*

WHERE TO FIND: Common summer resident (mid-May–September) of low-elevation riparian areas with dense, shrubby habitats north to Quesnel and Avola; rare at northern edge of region.

BEHAVIOUR: Forages mainly on the ground for insects and fruit. Nests on or near the ground in low shrubs.

DID YOU KNOW? Like the other members of this genus, this shy, beautiful thrush is heard far more often than it is seen.

DATE AND LOCATION SEEN: ______________________

____

____

DESCRIPTION: 18 cm. *Catharus* thrushes are plump, thin-billed birds with spotted breasts and buffy wing-stripes. Swainson's is **uniformly olive-brown** on the **upperparts**, **wings**, and **tail**. Has broad, **buff eye-ring**; **throat and breast** are **buffy with dark brown spots**; flanks are olive, belly is white.

SIMILAR SPECIES: Hermit Thrush (p. 317) has contrasting reddish tail, narrow white eye-ring. Veery (p. 313) has rusty-brown upperparts and faint spots on creamy breast.

VOICE: Call is low, liquid *bic,* also *bic-burr*; distinctive flutelike song spirals upward.

WHERE TO FIND: Common migrant (late May–June, August–September) and summer resident of low- to mid-elevation moist deciduous woodlands and coniferous forests with dense shrub understories, often in riparian areas.

BEHAVIOUR: Feeds on insects and fruit deep within shady woodland understory, sometimes more openly on pathways or edges. Secretive, heard much more often than seen.

DID YOU KNOW? Swainson's Thrushes migrate mainly at night, and their distinctive *queee* flight calls can be heard on quiet spring and fall evenings.

DATE AND LOCATION SEEN: ____________________

____

____

DESCRIPTION: 17 cm. Pale **brownish-grey above**, with **rump and tail contrastingly reddish-brown**. Buffy-white on **breast with blackish spots**; sides and flanks are greyish, belly is white. Has complete, **thin**, **white eye-ring**.

SIMILAR SPECIES: Swainson's Thrush (p. 315) lacks reddish tail and has buffy face pattern. Veery (p. 313) has reddish-brown upperparts and indistinct brown spots on buffy breast. Neither flicks wings or tail.

VOICE: Call is sharp *chup-chup*. Song begins with long clear whistle, then cascading flutelike whistles; successive songs are on different pitches.

WHERE TO FIND: Common migrant (April–May, September–November) and summer resident in mid- to high-elevation mature coniferous forests. Casual in winter in southern valleys.

BEHAVIOUR: Forages on the ground for insects, usually remaining in shade. Often visits fruiting shrubs. Usually seen singly. Rapidly flicks wings and slowly raises and lowers tail when perched.

DID YOU KNOW? Many birders consider this species the finest songster in North America.

DATE AND LOCATION SEEN: ______________________

____

____

Adult

Juvenile

DESCRIPTION: 25 cm. Familiar large, plump thrush with grey-brown upperparts, **rufous-red breast, and white markings around the eyes**. MALE: Head blackish, breast deep reddish-orange. FEMALE: Paler, duller with grey-brown head. JUVENILE: Heavily spotted on the breast, whitish on wings and back.

SIMILAR SPECIES: Varied Thrush (p. 321) has long orange eyebrow, grey or black breast band, orange patterning on wings.

VOICE: Song is pleasing carol of two- or three-note, rich whistled phrases. Calls include a hard *pup-pup*, a squealing *kli-kli-pup*, and a high thin contact call given when fledglings are present; similar to call of Cedar Waxwing. *BEEP* alarm call often given when mobbing an owl or other raptor.

WHERE TO FIND: Common migrant (February–March, September–October) and summer resident of moist woodlands and forests. In winter, they are common only in the Okanagan Valley, where they form flocks that wander widely in search of food sources.

BEHAVIOUR: In summer, feeds mainly on the ground for earth-worms and grubs. Winter flocks seek berries and fruit; often joining flocks of waxwings. Nest is a mud-lined open cup, usually placed in a crotch of a tree, but also on or in human structures where there is overhead protection.

DID YOU KNOW? Robins ground-forage by making short, fast, and halting runs to find worms and other prey. Occasionally the bird stops, cocks its head, and then pounces on a worm. Although it appears that robins are listening for their subterranean prey, a study in 1965 proved that they actually locate worms by sight.

DATE AND LOCATION SEEN: ____________________

____

____

Male
Female

DESCRIPTION: 24 cm. **Robin-like** thrush of mature, moist coniferous forests. Has **dark breast band**, **mask**, and **bill**; **orange eyebrow**, throat, wing patches and wing-bars. MALE: Has **bluish-grey** head, back, and tail; black mask and breast band. FEMALE: Faded version of male, with greyish upperparts and paler breast band.

SIMILAR SPECIES: American Robin (p. 319) has no breast band, eyebrow, or orange wing patches.

VOICE: Call is deep *chup*. Distinctive song is single, long buzzy whistle on one pitch followed every 10 seconds by similar note on a different pitch.

WHERE TO FIND: Fairly common summer resident (March–October) of moist coniferous forests, mostly at mid- to high elevations. Uncommon in winter in shrubby gullies in southern valleys, rare elsewhere.

BEHAVIOUR: Mostly forages through forest litter on the ground for insects and other invertebrates, also feeds on seeds and berries. Shy, most often seen in dark, shadowy habitats. Moves downslope in fall to winter in low-elevation riparian and coniferous forests.

DID YOU KNOW? The eerie, beautiful song of Varied Thrushes can be heard most often in early morning, late evening, or after a rain shower.

DATE AND LOCATION SEEN: ______________________________

____

____

DESCRIPTION: 22 cm. A **slate-grey bird** with a black crown. Has long, black tail and **rufous undertail**.

SIMILAR SPECIES: Female Brewer's Blackbird (p. 399) lacks black cap, rufous undertail.

VOICE: Call is hoarse, catlike mewing *maryyy*; also harsh chattering alarm call. Song is rambling, halting series of melodious, nasal, and squeaky notes and phrases interspersed with catlike *mew* notes.

WHERE TO FIND: Locally common summer resident (May–September) of low-elevation, dense riparian woodlands south of Williams Lake.

BEHAVIOUR: Forages mainly on the ground or close to it in very dense thickets for insects, seeds, and small fruits. Flight is typically low. Avoids crossing large openings and stays hidden in dense cover. Rises to a tall perch only to sing. Recognizes cowbird eggs and will eject them from the nest.

DID YOU KNOW? Gray Catbird often sings all night long, particularly on moonlit nights.

DATE AND LOCATION SEEN: ____________________

Sage Thrasher

Oreoscoptes montanus

DESCRIPTION: 22 cm. Medium-sized, **long-tailed** songbird of sage-brush country. **Upperparts light greyish-brown** with two fine, white wing-bars; **underparts whitish with crisp, dark streaking**; head has indistinct whitish eye-line and short, straight bill; tail is brownish grey with white corners.

SIMILAR SPECIES: Northern Mockingbird (rare) lacks crisp, dark streaking on underparts, has large white wing patches.

VOICE: Call is low *chup*; song is long, clear series of warbled phrases.

WHERE TO FIND: Rare migrant (April–June, August–September) and very local summer resident of sagebrush rangelands; almost all records are from the south Okanagan and lower Similkameen valleys. Best sites are White Lake in the south Okanagan and the Chopaka-Nighthawk border crossing in the south Similkameen.

BEHAVIOUR: Forages on the ground mostly for insects and other invertebrates, also eats berries if available. Builds its stick nest lined with sagebrush bark in large sagebrush. Sometimes builds shade platform over the nest.

DID YOU KNOW? The Sage Thrasher is listed as endangered in Canada because of its small distribution and threats to its habitat.

DATE AND LOCATION SEEN: ______________________

____

____

Juvenile
Breeding

Winter

DESCRIPTION: 22 cm. Stocky, **blackish** songbird with **short, squared tail** and pointed, brown wings. Has **straight, pointed bill**; dull pinkish-orange legs. BREEDING: Body plumage **iridescent black, bill bright yellow**. WINTER: Plumage **heavily spangled with whitish** spots, bill blackish; white spotting wears away in late winter to reveal breeding plumage. JUVENILE: Grey-brown all over, with dark bill and lores, but shows distinctive starling shape.

SIMILAR SPECIES: Brewer's Blackbird (p. 399) has longer tail, pale yellow eyes, and is unspotted.

VOICE: Calls include a buzzy *dzeeer*, harsh *shurrr*, and sharp *vit*. Extremely varied songs incorporate much mimicry. Buzzes, clicks, rattles, and high squealing characterize the prolonged song.

WHERE TO FIND: Common resident of open areas containing trees or buildings, especially in agricultural and residential areas, landfills; rare in northern part of region in winter.

BEHAVIOUR: Waddles on ground, using gaping motion of bill to probe lawns and soil. Flocks also exploit fruit, grain, and insects. Flies with rapid wingbeats, flight silhouette appearing triangular. Nests in trees or structure cavities, often aggressively usurping nest cavities from other birds. Gathers into large foraging flocks in late summer, fall, and winter.

DID YOU KNOW? This non-native species was introduced from Europe to New York in the late 1800s and arrived in British Columbia in 1945.

DATE AND LOCATION SEEN: ______________________

____

____

DESCRIPTION: 17 cm. Slender ground bird with a **thin bill**, grey-brown upperparts, pale, **buff-tinged underparts with streaks on the breast**, and **white outer tail feathers**. BREEDING: More grey above and richer buff below, with breast streaks reduced or absent. WINTER: More heavily streaked below, faintly streaked on back.

SIMILAR SPECIES: Larger Horned Lark (p. 271) has a black mask and throat and white-edged black tail. Many sparrows are somewhat similar, but have short, conical bills and do not bob tails.

VOICE: Common flight call a doubled *pi-pit*; also a thin *tseep*; song a loud series of musical *seedle* notes.

WHERE TO FIND: Common migrant (April–May, August–October) in open lowland areas. Fairly common summer resident of mountain alpine areas. Very rare in winter, mainly in Okanagan Valley.

BEHAVIOUR: Diet is mostly insects and some seeds. Walks on the ground, constantly bobbing tail. Post-breeding flocks forage in open fields, sometimes mixing with Horned Larks. Usually seen on the ground, but also perches on fence lines, wires, tree branches. Nests on ground in wet alpine areas with scattered rocks. Moves to lower elevations after nesting; forms large flocks in migration. Migrants prefer moist areas; often found on receding shorelines and in meadowlands.

DID YOU KNOW? In courtship flights, males fly high in the air, and then float downward while singing, holding their legs extended and tails cocked upward.

DATE AND LOCATION SEEN: ______________________

____

____

Cedar Waxwing
Adult
Cedar Waxwing
Juvenile

Bohemian Waxwing

Cedar Waxwing / Bohemian Waxwing

Bombycilla cedrorum / Bombycilla garrulus

DESCRIPTION: 18 cm/21 cm. **Crested** birds that travel in close flocks. CEDAR: **Soft brown above**, **tinged yellow on belly**; **black chin and mask**; lower back and rump grey. Blackish tail has **yellow band** at tip. Some have small, wax-like red spots on tips of inner flight feathers. BOHEMIAN: Similar to Cedar, but **larger and greyer**; has **greyish belly** and **rufous undertail**. **Wings** have **distinct yellow and white markings**.

SIMILAR SPECIES: European Starlings (p. 327) have similar flocking behaviour and triangular wing shape, but very different markings.

VOICE: CEDAR: Call is very high *sreeee*. BOHEMIAN: Call is like Cedar's, but somewhat lower-pitched and trilled.

WHERE TO FIND: CEDAR: Common summer residents (May–September) in forests, woodlands, and gardens throughout region, uncommon to rare in winter in residential areas. BOHEMIAN: Uncommon to abundant winter residents (November–April) of valleys and cities, found wherever plentiful sources of fruit exist. Uncommon summer residents in subalpine forests of plateaus and mountains, particularly the Chilcotin.

BEHAVIOUR: Both species share similar habits and often occur together. Gather in large flocks when not nesting and concentrate at prime foraging areas. Diet is mainly insects in summer, fruit and berries in fall and winter. Flocks often visit holly, juniper, mountain ash, and many other fruit-bearing ornamental plantings.

DID YOU KNOW? Both species habitually flycatch for insects along the wooded shores of rivers, lakes, and ponds.

DATE AND LOCATION SEEN: ______________________

____

____

Orange-crowned Warbler
Yellow

Orange-crowned Warble
Grey

Tennessee Warbler
Male

Tennessee Warbler
Immature

Vermivora celata / Vermivora peregrina

DESCRIPTION: 13 cm/12 cm. ORANGE-CROWNED: **Plain olive-yellow throughout**; with indistinct eyebrow, **yellowish eye-ring broken by thin, dark line through eye**; faint **olive breast streaking** and olive-grey tail. **Undertail coverts yellow**. Male has dull orange crown patch, usually hidden. TENNESSEE: Breeding male has **olive back, grey head with white eyebrow**, white below; female and young birds can be quite yellowish below, but **undertail coverts** are always **white**.

SIMILAR SPECIES: Yellow Warbler (p. 337) similar to bright Orange-crowned but lacks dark eye-line; has shorter tail with pale yellow areas, and pale yellow edges to wing feathers.

VOICE: ORANGE-CROWNED: Call is sharp *tik*; song is colourless trill that usually falls slightly in pitch at the end. TENNESSEE: Call is a high, sharp *stik*; song is a three-part series of high chips: *sip sip sip sip seeput seeput seeput seeput ti ti ti ti ti ti ti*.

WHERE TO FIND: ORANGE-CROWNED: Common migrant and summer resident (April–early October) in dense, brushy areas of meadows and open forests, including logging clearcuts. TENNESSEE: Uncommon summer resident (May–September) in deciduous and mixed spruce forests in northern third of region and through Rockies; rare migrant elsewhere.

BEHAVIOUR: Both nest on or near the ground.

DID YOU KNOW? Orange-crowned Warbler is often the most abundant species counted at migration monitoring stations in the region.

DATE AND LOCATION SEEN: ______________________

____

____

DESCRIPTION: 12 cm. Small, relatively short-tailed warbler with **olive upperparts**, mostly **yellow underparts including throat**. **Complete white eye-ring** on a **grey head.** Males have a distinctive but often hidden rufous crown patch.

SIMILAR SPECIES: MacGillivray's Warbler (p. 349) has a grey hood, including throat, and broken white eye-ring.

VOICE: Sharp *spink* call. Song is two-parted: a series of *seepa* notes followed by a short trill.

WHERE TO FIND: Common migrant (April–May, July–September) and summer resident in low- to mid-elevation dry coniferous and mixed forests with dense shrub understories. Often seen in shrubby clearcuts and riparian areas. Rare north of Williams Lake, Clearwater, and Golden.

BEHAVIOUR: Frequently bobs tail up and down while foraging. Gleans for insects and spiders in foliage of low shrubs and trees. Typical of warblers, males on territory may sing for many minutes from a high perch.

DID YOU KNOW? The Nashville species scientific name *ruficapilla* refers to the hidden rufous crown patch of males.

DATE AND LOCATION SEEN: ______________________

____

____

Male
Female

DESCRIPTION: 13 cm. Fairly stocky, **short-tailed** warbler that is **mainly yellow all over**. Plain head lacks markings except for a **bold, dark eye** and indistinct pale eye-ring. MALE: Bright yellow, with **thin red streaks on the breast**. FEMALE: More dull and pale, and lacking red streaks. Immature females can be very dull grey, nearly lacking yellow. All birds show yellow patches in tail (**tail appears all yellow below**), yellow or whitish edges to wing feathers.

SIMILAR SPECIES: Orange-crowned (p. 333) and Wilson's Warblers (p. 353) have longer, all-dark tails.

VOICE: Call is loud, down-slurred *chip*; sprightly song starts with high sweet notes, then a short twitter and an emphatic ending *see-see-whew*.

WHERE TO FIND: Common migrant (April–May, August–September) and summer resident of brushy riparian woodlands and thickets.

BEHAVIOUR: Employs typical warbler gleaning behaviour while foraging for insects, sometimes high in deciduous trees. Forms fairly large flocks during migration, when it often uses more varied habitats. Nest is built low in a bush or small tree.

DID YOU KNOW? As with many of our riparian species, Yellow Warbler nests are often parasitized by Brown-headed Cowbirds, but the warbler can recognize cowbird eggs and re-nest. They sometimes simply build a new nest on top of the old one, burying the previously laid eggs.

DATE AND LOCATION SEEN: ______________________________

____

____

Male
Immature

MAGNOLIA WARBLER

Dendroica tigrina

DESCRIPTION: 13 cm. Distinctive warbler of moister coniferous and mixed forests. Bright yellow below with **heavy black streaks** on sides; grey above, white eyebrow. **Large white tail spots** and white undertail coverts. MALE: Has black mask, large white wing patch. FEMALE: Has olive-green ear patch and crown with little black on the throat. IMMATURE: Lacks black stripes on side and white eyebrow, has pale grey neckband.

SIMILAR SPECIES: Townsend's Warbler (p. 343) has yellow face.

VOICE: Call is nasal *vint*; songs are variable; short, musical phrase like *sweeter sweeter SWEETEST*; like weak Redstart call.

WHERE TO FIND: Fairly common summer resident (May-September) in moist coniferous and mixed forests, especially spruce forests, in northeastern quarter of region (Cariboo Mountains, northern Monashees, Selkirks, and Rockies); rare migrant elsewhere. Can be found in Wells Gray and Mount Robson Provincial Parks.

BEHAVIOUR: Gleans insects from conifer needles and deciduous leaves.

DID YOU KNOW? Magnolia Warbler populations are stable or increasing, probably because bird does well in young forests, both on breeding and wintering grounds.

DATE AND LOCATION SEEN: ____________________

Audubon's
Male
Audubon's
Female

Myrtle
Male
Myrtle
Female

DESCRIPTION: 14 cm. Region's most abundant warbler has **bright yellow rump patch**, **yellow patch on sides**, and **white tail spots**. Grey to grey-brown, with white wing-bars and whitish belly. Audubon's subspecies has **yellow throat patch** (may be whitish in immature females); breeding male has black chest, large white wing patch. Myrtle subspecies has white throat, which extends back to point behind ear region, and whitish eyebrow; breeding male has mottled black chest and bold white wing-bars.

SIMILAR SPECIES: Yellow rump patch distinguishes even the dullest immatures from other regularly seen warblers.

VOICE: Audubon's call is loud *chip* and Myrtle gives a flatter *chep*; song is loosely patterned warble.

WHERE TO FIND: Common and widespread migrants (March–May, August–October). Rare in winter in southern valleys. Audubon's is common summer resident of open, dry coniferous forests and mixed woodlands with considerable ground foliage. Myrtle breeds north of region in British Columbia and east of Rockies; elsewhere an uncommon to rare migrant.

BEHAVIOUR: Feeds by gleaning foliage, flycatching, hovering, or searching on the ground. Diet is mainly insects, but also includes fruit. Noted as one of the last warblers to leave its breeding grounds in fall, and one of the first to return in spring. Often forages in large flocks during migration.

DID YOU KNOW? The Audubon's and Myrtle subspecies were formerly regarded as separate species.

DATE AND LOCATION SEEN: ______________________

____

____

Male
Female

DESCRIPTION: 13 cm. Distinctive warbler of moister coniferous forests. Has **yellow and dark head pattern** with **yellow arc below eye**, **yellow breast with dark flank streaking**, olive-green upperparts, dark wings with two bold white wing-bars, white belly. MALE: Has black on the throat, ear patch, and much of the crown. Immature males are similar but have less black. FEMALE: Has olive-green ear patch and crown with little black on the throat. The dullest females lack black throats and are pale yellow on the throat and breast.

SIMILAR SPECIES: Black-throated Gray Warbler (rare on eastern edge of region) is similar, but is white instead of yellow on the face and breast. Black-throated Green Warbler (rare on eastern slopes of Rockies) has plain green back, duller face pattern, and less yellow on breast.

VOICE: Call is high *tip*; songs are variable but always high, thin, buzzy, and usually rising, such as *zee zee zee zee zeeeeee zeeta-zee* or *zeezeezeezee ZEE slip*.

WHERE TO FIND: Common migrant (May–June, August–October), summer resident of mature mid-elevation coniferous forests.

BEHAVIOUR: Actively gleans, hover-gleans, and flycatches insects in the upper portion of tree canopy. Males sing from the tops of tall trees. Joins mixed-species flocks in migration.

DID YOU KNOW? Townsend's Warblers interbreed extensively with Hermit Warblers in the Cascade Mountains south of this region, and also with Black-throated Green Warblers northwest of this region.

DATE AND LOCATION SEEN: ____________________

____

____

Blackpoll Warbler
Male
Blackpoll Warbler
Immature
American Redstart
Male
American Redstart
Female

DESCRIPTION: 14 cm/13 cm. BLACKPOLL: **Striped black**, **white**, **and grey** over much of body; **yellow legs and feet**. Breeding male has **black cap**, **white face**, and heavy black streaks on sides. Non-breeding adults and immatures can be **quite yellow** on head and breast, immatures only faintly streaked. REDSTART: MALE: **Mostly black** except for white belly and **orange sides**, **wing-bars**, **and tail flashes**. FEMALE: Patterned like male, but black is replaced by light grey on head, back is light grey to green. Sides, wing-bars, and tail base are yellow.

SIMILAR SPECIES: Redstart unmistakable. Non-breeding Blackpolls can resemble young Townsend's Warblers (p. 343), but lack strong facial pattern; no other warbler has yellow legs and feet.

VOICE: BLACKPOLL: Call is a sharp *chip*; song is very high-pitched series of notes, loudest in the middle: *sisisiSISISISISISSsisisisi*. REDSTART: Call is high *tsip*; songs variable, but include a high *tsee tsee tsee tsee tswee* and *teetsa teetsa teetsa seet.*

WHERE TO FIND: BLACKPOLL: Uncommon to fairly common summer resident (May-September) in wet spruce woodlands north of Quesnel, farther south in Rockies. REDSTART: Rare to common migrant (May-June, August-September) and summer resident; more common in moister forests north of the Thompson River. Favours deciduous forest with abundant shrubs.

BEHAVIOUR: Diet of both species is mainly insects caught by gleaning and flycatching.

DID YOU KNOW? It is thought that redstarts flash their wing and tail patches when foraging to flush out insects hidden in the foliage.

DATE AND LOCATION SEEN: ______

Northern Waterthrush

Seiurus noveboracensis

DESCRIPTION: 15 cm. Skulking warbler of willow tangles, wooded swamps, and beaver ponds. Dark brown above, white below, **heavily striped** with black, obvious white eyebrow. Some birds have yellow tinge on belly. Legs are pink. **Habitually bobs tail**.

SIMILAR SPECIES: Song Sparrow (p. 375) has shorter, thicker bill, longer tail, does not bob. Ovenbird (east of Rockies) is olive-green above, has black and orange crown stripes, and is found in deciduous woodlands, not wetlands.

VOICE: Call is loud, hard *spik*; song is loud, clear, three-parted series, each section usually lower than the previous: *sweet sweet sweet weet weet weet chu chu chu.*

WHERE TO FIND: Fairly common summer resident (mid-May-September) around wooded swamps, beaver ponds, and other forested wetlands with thick willows and other shrubs. Inconspicuous in migration.

BEHAVIOUR: Forages deep in brushy tangles along wooded shorelines. Nests on ground, usually in root tangles of upturned stumps or fern clumps on banks.

DID YOU KNOW? Northern Waterthrushes are almost always detected by their song.

DATE AND LOCATION SEEN: ______________________________

____

____

Male
Female

DESCRIPTION: 13 cm. Skulking warbler of dense thickets. **Olive-green above** and **yellow below**. **Head, throat, and breast are mostly grey** (appears **dark-hooded**) with **prominent white arcs above and below the eyes**. Bill is relatively long and bicoloured (blackish above, pinkish below) and legs are long and pinkish. MALE: Hood is dark grey, darkest in front of eyes and across breast. FEMALE, IMMATURE: Hood is pale grey, lightest (sometimes whitish) on throat.

SIMILAR SPECIES: Nashville Warbler (p. 335) has yellow throat and complete eye-ring. Orange-crowned Warbler (p. 333) lacks defined grey hood, has blurry breast streaking. Mourning Warbler (east of Rockies) is very similar; lacks white arcs above and below eyes.

VOICE: Call is hard, sharp *chik*; song is short series *sweet-sweet-sweet, sugar, sugar,* somewhat burrier and rougher than other similar warbler songs.

WHERE TO FIND: Fairly common migrant (May–June, August–September) and summer resident of mid- to high-elevation moist brushy areas.

BEHAVIOUR: Gleans for insects close to the ground in moist, dense shrubby places, mainly riparian areas and cutover forests.

DID YOU KNOW? This species had originally been called Tolmie's Warbler by John Kirk Townsend in honour of Dr. W.T. Tolmie, the surgeon at Fort Vancouver, Washington. It was renamed MacGillivray's Warbler by John James Audubon in honour of his Scottish editor, Dr. William MacGillivray.

DATE AND LOCATION SEEN: ______________________

____

____

Male
Immature

Common Yellowthroat
Geothlypis trichas

DESCRIPTION: 13 cm. A skulking, marsh-dwelling warbler. **Bright yellow throat** contrasts with duller **flanks washed with brownish**. Upperparts olive-green; undertail yellow. MALE: **Bold black mask and forehead** bordered behind by white. FEMALE: Lacks mask, has indistinct whitish eye-ring; yellow throat contrasts with brownish cheeks and flanks. Young males have faint black face mask.

SIMILAR SPECIES: Female Yellow (p. 337), Nashville (p. 335), Orange-crowned (p. 333), and MacGillivray's Warblers (p. 349) are similar, but lack Yellowthroat's strong contrast between yellow throat and dull, pale brownish underparts, and indistinct complete eye-ring.

VOICE: Call is husky *tidge*; distinctive, loud song is *wich-i-ty wich-i-ty wich-i-ty.*

WHERE TO FIND: Common migrant and summer resident (April–September) of marshes, wet meadows, and other wetlands with dense, emergent vegetation, usually bulrushes. Migrants often use dense, brushy habitats.

BEHAVIOUR: Gleans insects and spiders in bulrushes or dense shrubby vegetation. Male sings from an open perch, and sometimes gives song in short flights. Builds loose, bulky nest on or near the ground.

DID YOU KNOW? Along with Yellow Warbler, this is the most widespread warbler in North America.

DATE AND LOCATION SEEN: ______________________

____

____

Male
Female

DESCRIPTION: 12 cm. A small, active warbler that is **bright yellow-olive above** and **bright golden-yellow below**. The yellow forehead contrasts with a **shiny black crown** (males) or mixed black and olive crown in most females (some females show only olive). The dark eye stands out on the blank yellow face. The wings and tail are unmarked olive-green.

SIMILAR SPECIES: Yellow Warbler (p. 337) is plumper and shorter tailed, has yellow tail spots and edges to wing feathers. Orange-crowned Warbler (p. 333) is much duller olive-yellow overall and has yellowish eye-ring broken by thin dark line through the eye.

VOICE: Call is distinctive, soft *timp*. Song is rapid series of *chip* notes, building in volume and speed, but often trailing off at the end.

WHERE TO FIND: Common migrant (April–May, August–September) and summer resident of mid- to high-elevation coniferous forests with shrub thickets in riparian and wet areas. Found in a wider variety of well-vegetated habitats during migration.

BEHAVIOUR: Intensely active, gleaning, hovering, and making short sallies for flying insects, mostly close to the ground. The tail is flipped as the bird flits about. Nests on or near the ground in dense understory vegetation.

DID YOU KNOW? Along with the phalarope, snipe, plover, and storm-petrel, this is one of the birds named for famed late 18th- and early 19th-century American ornithologist Alexander Wilson.

DATE AND LOCATION SEEN: ______________________________

____

____

Yellow-breasted Chat

Icteria virens

DESCRIPTION: 19 cm. **Large**, **thick-billed** warbler-like bird with **deep yellow throat and breast**, **white spectacles** around the eyes, olive upperparts, whitish belly, and a **long olive tail**. The sexes are similar, but females have less black in front of eye and less intensely yellow breast.

SIMILAR SPECIES: Common Yellowthroat (p. 351) is much smaller and lacks white spectacles.

VOICE: Call is nasal *airrh* and a snappy *jeew*. Loud, rich song is distinctive, consisting of loose collection of chatters, rattles, caws, and whistles with notes sometimes repeated rapidly.

WHERE TO FIND: Rare and local migrant and summer resident (May–September) of dense riparian thickets in southern valleys. Most easily found in the south Okanagan region, but also breeds regularly in the Columbia Valley south of Trail. Inconspicuous in migration.

BEHAVIOUR: Skulks, sings, and forages in dense shrubs and thickets. Territorial male sometimes perches openly for prolonged periods while singing, or sings exuberantly in flight with deep wingbeats. Feeds on insects and berries.

DID YOU KNOW? The relationship of Yellow-breasted Chats to other wood-warblers continues to be studied and debated. It now appears that this species is only distantly related to our more typical warblers.

DATE AND LOCATION SEEN: ______________________

____

____

Male
Female

DESCRIPTION: 18 cm. **Bill** is **stout** compared to slender, pointed bills of orioles, but not conical like those of grosbeaks. MALE: Has red to **orange-red head**; otherwise **bright yellow** with **black back, wings, and tail**, two wing-bars (front yellow, rear white). FEMALE: Olive-green to olive-grey above, pale yellow below, with **two white wing-bars**; some show only limited yellow on underparts, dark tail. Immature males have less orange on face.

SIMILAR SPECIES: Female Bullock's Oriole (p. 403) has thinner, more pointed, darker bill, yellow tail.

VOICE: Call is rising *br-d-dik*; song is a rapid series of hoarse, scratchy robin-like phrases: *pr-rit, pre-ur-rit, pree-u.*

WHERE TO FIND: Common migrant (May–June, July–September) and summer resident of open coniferous and mixed forests.

BEHAVIOUR: Gleans insects with sluggish movements through foliage, often high in trees; sallies after flying insects such as dragonflies. Also eats berries in late summer and fall.

DID YOU KNOW? Recent DNA studies suggest that North American tanagers are more closely related to Black-headed Grosbeaks and Lazuli Buntings than to the diverse tanagers of the New World tropics.

DATE AND LOCATION SEEN: ____________________

____

____

Adult
Juvenile

Spotted Towhee
Pipilo maculatus

DESCRIPTION: 22 cm. Large sparrow with **black hood**, **white-spotted black wings** and back, and white corners on black tail. Bright **rufous sides**, flanks, and undertail, contrasting with white centre breast and belly. **Eyes are red**. Female is slightly duller, with slate grey head. Juvenile is brownish and heavily streaked, has distinctive wing spotting and white tail corners.

SIMILAR SPECIES: Dark-eyed Junco (p. 383) is smaller, lacks white spots and rufous sides. Smaller size, lack of white tail corners separate streaked sparrows from juvenile towhee.

VOICE: Call is harsh, rising mew *hreee-eee*. Song is loud, buzzy trill *che zheeeeee*.

WHERE TO FIND: Common summer resident of shrubby habitats at low elevations in valleys south of Williams Lake. Uncommon to rare in winter in southern valleys, usually at feeders.

BEHAVIOUR: Forages and nests in dense, brushy areas.

DID YOU KNOW? Towhees employ "double scratch" foraging, a quick one-hop forward, one-hop backward manoeuvre that turns over leaves and other ground debris to expose hidden food items.

DATE AND LOCATION SEEN: ______________________________

American Tree Sparrow

Spizella arborea

DESCRIPTION: 16 cm. **Long-tailed**, round-headed wintering sparrow of open country. Has grey head with a **rufous crown** and eye-line. Upperparts are streaked rusty-brown with two **white wing-bars.** Underparts are pale grey with a **prominent dark central breast spot** and buff sides. Upper bill is dark grey, lower is yellow.

SIMILAR SPECIES: Larger immature White-crowned Sparrow (p. 379) lacks a central breast spot, has all pale bill. Chipping Sparrow (p. 363; not present in winter) lacks a breast spot, has white line over the eye.

VOICE: Call is clear, soft *tseet* and *tsidle-eet.*

WHERE TO FIND: Uncommon and local winter (October–March) resident in southern valleys. Antelope-brush grassland at the north end of Osoyoos Lake is perhaps the most reliable spot.

BEHAVIOUR: Forages mainly for seeds and invertebrates in willow riparian areas, brushy roadsides, fields, and hedgerows. Regularly perches on fencelines and small trees, but seldom high off the ground. Usually seen in small post-breeding flocks.

DID YOU KNOW? American Tree Sparrows are common breeding birds at the treeline in northern British Columbia.

DATE AND LOCATION SEEN: ______________________

____

____

Adult
Juvenile

DESCRIPTION: 14 cm. Small, slim, long-tailed sparrow with grey underparts and rump, and streaked brown back. BREEDING: Distinctive face pattern: **black eye-line**, **white eyebrow**, and **rufous crown**; bill is black. NON-BREEDING: Crown is finely streaked and brownish, bill is dull pinkish, **rump grey**. Juvenile is like dull non-breeding adult, but extensively streaked below.

SIMILAR SPECIES: Brewer's Sparrow (p. 365) has finely streaked crown, pale area between bill and eye, and thin white eye-ring. Clay-coloured Sparrow (p. 365) has brown rump, dark streaks on crown; American Tree Sparrow (p. 361) has a central breast spot.

VOICE: Call includes rich *tseet* and soft *tik*. Song is dry trill, usually faster and less musical than similar song of Dark-eyed Junco.

WHERE TO FIND: Common migrant (April–May, August–October) and summer resident of dry, open coniferous forests.

BEHAVIOUR: Mainly forages for small seeds, fruits, and insects on the ground in grassy forest understory. Sings from elevated perch, and flies into trees when disturbed. Places finely woven nest in shrub or tree. Forms flocks in migration, often with other sparrow species.

DID YOU KNOW? They are among the most widespread sparrows in North America, breeding from Alaska to Nicaragua.

DATE AND LOCATION SEEN: ______________________________

____

____

Brewer's Sparrow
Clay-colored Sparrow

Brewer's Sparrow / Clay-colored Sparrow

Spizella breweri / Spizella pallida

DESCRIPTION: 14 cm. BREWER'S: Slender, pale, **long-tailed** sparrow with **finely streaked crown**, **narrow whitish eye-ring**, streaked greyish-brown upperparts, and **unstreaked pale-grey lowerparts**. CLAY-COLORED: Very similar to Brewer's, but has **two dark stripes** on either side of crown with central pale stripe; **light brown face boldly outlined** in dark brown.

SIMILAR SPECIES: Immature Chipping Sparrow (p. 363) is darker, with strong dark eye-line, grey rump.

VOICE: BREWER'S**:** Call is thin *tsip*; song is long, distinctive, descending series of buzzy, varied, canary-like trills. CLAY-COLORED: Song is a short series of dry buzzes on one pitch; call similar to Brewer's.

WHERE TO FIND: BREWER'S: Locally common summer resident (April-September) of sagebrush grasslands in southern Okanagan Valley; timberline subspecies uncommon in subalpine shrubs of Rocky Mountains. Rare migrant elsewhere. CLAY-COLORED: Uncommon to rare and local summer resident in thick shrubs (rose, snowberry) in grasslands throughout region.

BEHAVIOUR: Both species forage on the ground and in low shrubs for insects and seeds. Build nests low in shrubs.

DID YOU KNOW? The sagebrush and timberline subspecies of the Brewer's Sparrow are sometimes considered separate species.

DATE AND LOCATION SEEN: ______________________

____

____

VESPER SPARROW

Pooecetes gramineus

DESCRIPTION: 16 cm. Common, **fairly large**, streaky sparrow of dry grasslands and open ponderosa pine forests. **White outer tail feathers** visible in flight. Upperparts are entirely dark-streaked greyish-brown and underparts are creamy white with **fine dark streaks on the breast** and flanks. Has unstreaked belly; head patterned brown and tan; shows thin **white eye-ring**. **Small chestnut patch at bend of wing** is not always visible.

SIMILAR SPECIES: Savannah Sparrow (p. 371) has distinct eyebrow, lacks eye-ring and white outer tail feathers, and has broad streaking on the flanks. Lapland Longspur (p. 385) has broad chestnut wing patch and bold eyebrow.

VOICE: Call is sharp *chirp*; song consists of two clear whistles followed by series of short, descending trills.

WHERE TO FIND: Uncommon to common migrant (April–May, August–September) and summer resident of dry, open grasslands, pastures, and sagebrush.

BEHAVIOUR: Forages mainly for seeds and insects on the ground. Nest cup placed on ground, protected by grass clump or small shrub. Males sing from highest exposed perch in their territories, often fence posts or tall shrubs. Breeding males also give short flight songs. Migrates in small flocks.

DID YOU KNOW? When they feel threatened, female Vesper Sparrows pretend they are injured and scurry away from their nests dragging a wing to lure the intruder away.

DATE AND LOCATION SEEN: ______________________

____

____

DESCRIPTION: 17 cm. Large, handsomely marked sparrow of open, arid country. **Bold face pattern** includes chestnut ear patch with white spot at rear, black whiskers, white markings around eyes, and chestnut and white crown stripes. Whitish below with **black spot in centre of breast**. Long, **rounded tail has bold white outer edge and corners**. IMMATURE: Slightly duller on head.

SIMILAR SPECIES: Smaller Chipping Sparrow (p. 363) has red crown, lacks bold face pattern and white tail corners. Vesper Sparrow (p. 367) lacks bold head pattern, has eye-ring and streaked breast. Has white only on edges of tail.

VOICE: Call is sharp warbler-like *tsip*. Complex song consists of varied short phrases, often repeated two to four times and includes sweet notes and rough, burry trills.

WHERE TO FIND: Uncommon migrant (April–May, August–September) and summer resident of south Okanagan and lower Similkameen valleys; rare in north Okanagan and Shuswap, very rare elsewhere in region. Frequents lower elevation open areas, usually grasslands with large shrubs, including sagebrush and antelope-brush habitats, or open ponderosa pine forests.

BEHAVIOUR: Feeds on insects and seeds in short-grass areas. Flies with strong, undulating wingbeats. Has elaborate courtship display and nests on the ground or in small shrubs.

DID YOU KNOW? Lark Sparrows are associated with grassland habitats with bare earth between grass clumps and shrubs, so may actually benefit from cattle grazing.

DATE AND LOCATION SEEN: ____________________

Savannah Sparrow

Grasshopper Sparrow

Savannah Sparrow / Grasshopper Sparrow

Passerculus sandwichensis / Ammodramus savannarum

DESCRIPTION: 14 cm/13 cm. SAVANNAH: **Small** sparrow of open areas, with **streaked** back, **breast**, and **flanks**; often has yellowish or white eyebrow. Has small bill, **short**, **notched tail**, and **bright pink legs**. GRASSHOPPER: **Unstreaked buffy below**, streaked rufous and brown above. Has relatively **large**, **flat head**; **eyebrow** that is **orangish in front**, **grey behind**; **dark crown with pale central stripe**; **long bill**; and short tail.

SIMILAR SPECIES: Song Sparrow (p. 375) has longer, rounded tail and greyer face; Vesper Sparrow (p. 367) has white outer tail feathers.

VOICE: SAVANNAH: Call is high, sharp *tick*; song is high *sip sip sip tseeeeeeee sirrrr.* GRASSHOPPER: Call is very high, sharp *tipip*; song is very high, insect-like *tip tup seeeeeeeee.*

WHERE TO FIND: SAVANNAH: Common migrant (April–May, August–September) and summer resident of pastures and moist grasslands. GRASSHOPPER: Rare and local summer resident (April–September) of native grasslands in Okanagan Valley. Reliable sites include White Lake; dry grasslands at the north end of Osoyoos Lake; and Goose Lake, Vernon.

BEHAVIOUR: Both species forage for insects and seeds, and nest on the ground. Savannah Sparrows often form large flocks in migration. Grasshopper Sparrows are loosely colonial.

DID YOU KNOW? Grasshopper Sparrows escape intruders by scurrying through the grass like mice, flying only when necessary.

DATE AND LOCATION SEEN: ______________________

____

____

DESCRIPTION: 18 cm. Large, stocky sparrow with a **grey head** and upperparts; **rusty wings and tail**; coarse, dark flank streaking, and white **breast with spots like inverted Vs or chevrons.** Bill has conspicuous **yellow lower mandible.**

SIMILAR SPECIES: Much smaller Song Sparrow (p. 375) has striped face and head, streaked back and all-dark bill.

VOICE: Call is metallic *chink*; song is clear and ringing, with slurred musical notes.

WHERE TO FIND: Uncommon migrant (April–May, August–October) throughout region, fairly common summer resident in subalpine forests and meadows at high elevations. Very rare in winter in southern valleys.

BEHAVIOUR: Scratches on the ground for seeds and insects. Builds nest on the ground or in a low shrub.

DID YOU KNOW? Four distinct groups of Fox Sparrows have been recognized across their extensive breeding range, and some experts consider these four to be separate species. Three of the four groups breed in British Columbia. The grey-headed "Slate-coloured" is the common breeding bird in the Interior mountains. The coastal "Sooty" group is uniformly dark brown. The boreal "Red" Fox Sparrows, which breed north of this region and are rare in migration, are rufous overall with a grey pattern on the face and grey streaks on the back.

DATE AND LOCATION SEEN: ______________________

____

____

Song Sparrow
Melospiza melodia

DESCRIPTION: 16 cm. Common and familiar long-tailed sparrow of wet, brushy areas. Dark brown all over, **boldly streaked below**, often with an irregular dark central breast spot. Strongly patterned face with **broad**, **grey eyebrow** and black whisker stripe. The **wings and tail are tinged rusty**. JUVENILE: More lightly streaked, with buffy wash below.

SIMILAR SPECIES: Larger Fox Sparrow (p. 373) has yellow lower mandible; lacks bold face pattern and streaked back. Smaller Lincoln's Sparrow (p. 377) is more finely streaked and has buffy breast. Savannah Sparrow (p. 371) is paler brown, has short, notched tail, bright pink legs, and usually has yellowish eyebrow.

VOICE: Call is distinctive *chimp*; song is variable series of trills following several short, sharp notes.

WHERE TO FIND: Common resident of low-elevation riparian woodlands, and other wet, densely vegetated habitats, including residential areas. Some breed at higher elevations, but move to lower elevations in winter. Very rare in winter at northern end of region.

BEHAVIOUR: Diet is varied, but consists mostly of insects, seeds, and berries. Singing males may perch openly for many minutes, but otherwise they forage low, often on the ground. Nests on the ground or low in a shrub.

DID YOU KNOW? Over two dozen subspecies of this geographically variable sparrow have been recognized, but research indicates that all are genetically similar.

DATE AND LOCATION SEEN: ______________________

____

____

DESCRIPTION: 14.5 cm. Skulking sparrow of dense, wet, shrubby areas. **Breast is washed with buff** and is **finely streaked**. Also has broad, grey eyebrow, narrow buff eye-ring, and **buffy whisker mark**. Wings are tinged rusty. Slender and long-tailed, with **peaked crown**.

SIMILAR SPECIES: Song Sparrow (p. 375) is larger, more boldly streaked and lacks buffy breast; has very different call.

VOICE: Call is sharp *tuk*. Song is hurried, rollicking warble, usually rising and then falling in pitch.

WHERE TO FIND: Common migrant (April–May, September–October) and summer resident of wet sedge meadows, bogs, and thickets. Common but usually inconspicuous visitor to lowland brushy areas during migration. Very rare in winter in southern valleys.

BEHAVIOUR: Forages on the ground under cover for insects and seeds. Moves furtively through low, dense, weedy growth and damp brushy areas.

DID YOU KNOW? This sparrow was named by Audubon in 1833, not for Honest Abe but for Thomas Lincoln, his assistant on a field trip to Labrador.

DATE AND LOCATION SEEN: ______________________

____

____

White-crowned Sparrow Adult

White-crowned Sparrow Immature

White-throated Sparrow

White-crowned Sparrow / White-throated Sparrow

Zonotrichia leucophrys / Zonotrichia albicollis

DESCRIPTION: 18 cm/17 cm. Fairly large, long-tailed sparrows with unstreaked grey breasts and greyish-brown upperparts. WHITE-CROWNED: Has **bold black-and-white crown stripes**; grey underparts; pinkish bill. In immatures, crown stripes are dark brown and grey with buff crown centre. WHITE-THROATED: Similar to White-crown, but with **clearly marked white throat**, rusty-brown upperparts, and **bright yellow spot in front of eye**.

SIMILAR SPECIES: Golden-crowned Sparrow (p. 381) has yellow crown thickly bordered by black, and a darker bill.

VOICE: WHITE-CROWNED: Call is sharp *pink*, song is clear whistles followed by buzzes and trills, rises then falls at end: see see zeezee zee. WHITE-THROATED: Call a metallic *chink*; song is diagnostic, pure whistle: *Oh sweet Canada Canada Canada.*

WHERE TO FIND: WHITE-CROWNED: Common migrant (April-May, August-November), passing through in huge flocks in late April and early May; uncommon summer resident of mid- to high-elevation brushy meadows and dense shrublands. Uncommon to fairly common in winter, mainly in the southern valleys; rare elsewhere. WHITE-THROATED: Rare to uncommon migrant and winter resident, usually with White-crowned and Golden-crowned Sparrows; common summer resident in mixed woodlands north of Quesnel.

BEHAVIOUR: Both species forage on the ground for insects, seeds, and fruit in brushy areas, and fly into dense cover when flushed.

DID YOU KNOW? Unlike many songbirds, both species often sing at night on their breeding grounds.

DATE AND LOCATION SEEN: ______________________

____

____

Golden-crowned Sparrow
Adult

Golden-crowned Sparro
Immature

Harris's Sparrow
Adult

Harris's Sparrow
Immature

DESCRIPTION: 18 cm/19 cm. **Large** sparrows. GOLDEN-CROWNED: **Dull grey below**, with streaked brownish back, dull pinkish-grey bill, and a **yellow patch on the forecrown**. Adult's crown is bordered with black; forehead is bright yellow (pattern bolder in breeding plumage, with black extending down to eyes). Immature's head is plainer, with dull yellow tinge to forehead. HARRIS'S: Adult has **black crown and throat**, grey (breeding) or buff (non-breeding) face, **white underparts with dark-streaked flanks**, streaked brownish back, **pink bill**, grey (adult) or buff face. Immature is like non-breeding adult, except crown is brownish and throat is white with dark brown necklace.

SIMILAR SPECIES: Smaller immature White-crowned Sparrow (p. 379) lacks yellow on crown.

VOICE: GOLDEN-CROWNED: Call is slurred *chink*. Song is three or more whistled notes: "Oh dear me." HARRIS'S: Call is loud *chip*.

WHERE TO FIND: GOLDEN-CROWNED: Summer resident of sub-alpine forests in northern Rocky Mountains. Uncommon migrant (September–October, April–May) throughout region and rare winter resident of lowland riparian woodlands in southern valleys. HARRIS'S: Rare migrant and winter resident, mainly in southern valleys.

BEHAVIOUR: GOLDEN-CROWNED: Makes short-distance migrations from Rocky Mountains to nearby lowlands in fall; most winter on Pacific coast. HARRIS'S: Migrates mainly east of the Rocky Mountains.

DID YOU KNOW? In our region these beautiful sparrows are usually discovered among White-crowned Sparrow flocks.

DATE AND LOCATION SEEN: ______________________

____

____

Oregon
Male
Oregon
Female
Oregon
Juvenile
Slate-coloured

DESCRIPTION: 15 cm. **Dark-hooded sparrow** with **light pink bill** and **flashing white outer tail feathers**. Two main forms in region. "Oregon" male has **black head** contrasting with **pinkish-brown back**, white chest, and **pinkish sides**. Female's head colour ranges from slate-grey to pale grey. "Slate-coloured" birds have slate- or grey-brown backs and slate-grey sides (paler and washed with brown in females). All juveniles are streaked brown above and below.

SIMILAR SPECIES: Immature juncos similar to Vesper Sparrow (p. 367), but are darker, lack the sparrow's facial pattern and have pink bills.

VOICE: Call is high, hard *stip*; song is simple, musical trill.

WHERE TO FIND: Common summer residents of forests at all elevations, also common migrants and winter residents (September–May) of low-elevation valleys. Very common at winter feeders in southern valleys, rare at northern end of region.

BEHAVIOUR: Forages on the ground for insects and seeds. Nests are almost always constructed on the ground on a sloping bank or rock face, often hidden in depressions, under grasses, or other cover.

DID YOU KNOW? The "Oregon" form breeds through most of the region; "Slate-coloured" form breeds in northern BC and along east slope of Rockies, migrates through and winters in the rest of the region. Until 1973, these two forms were considered separate species.

DATE AND LOCATION SEEN: ______________________

____

____

Snow Bunting
Male

Snow Bunting
Female

Lapland Longspur
Breeding

Lapland Longspur
Non-breeding

DESCRIPTION: 17 cm/16 cm. Small Arctic songbirds that migrate through and winter in open fields. Have conical bills like their sparrow relatives. BUNTING: Has largely **white wings with black tips**. Breeding male is **white all over** with **black back**, and black and white wings and tail. Breeding female like male, but with greyish head and rufous streaking on back. Non-breeding birds have white underparts with rusty breast band, **rusty patches on head** and flanks. LONGSPUR: All plumages have mottled rust and brown upperparts, **rusty wing patch**, streaked flanks, white belly, and dark brown **tail with white outer feathers**. Breeding male has **black head** with white frame, black breast, rufous nape, and black flank streaks. Females and immatures have rusty heads with **dark ear patch**.

SIMILAR SPECIES: Horned Lark (p. 271) has solid brown back and wings; long, mostly black tail.

VOICE: BUNTING: Call is clear, descending *cheew*, and a soft, husky rattle. LONGSPUR: Distinctive calls are a husky *deeew* and dry rattle *trididit*.

WHERE TO FIND: Uncommon to rare migrants and winter residents (November–March) in open country.

BEHAVIOUR: Both species forage on ground for seeds in grasslands, alpine tundra, plowed or sparsely vegetated fields.

DID YOU KNOW? These species get their striking breeding plumage through feather wear. They do not moult in spring; the breeding colour pattern is hidden in the winter plumage by dull brown feather tips that wear off in spring to reveal the pattern below.

DATE AND LOCATION SEEN: ______________________________

____

____

Male

Female

DESCRIPTION: 21 cm. **Very thick**, **conical bicoloured bill**; **white wing patterning and yellow underwing linings** are distinctive in all plumages. ADULT: **Male's head** is **mostly black**; back streaked; **collar**, **breast**, **sides**, **and rump rich orange**; black wings and tail have bold white markings. IMMATURE: Male is duller, with striped head. Female has **brown crown stripes** and eye-line; **tawny**, **streaked breast**; brown wings with few white markings.

SIMILAR SPECIES: Very similar female Rose-breasted Grosbeak (rare) has distinctly streaked whitish breast and pink underwings (yellow in Black-headed).

VOICE: Call is sharp *pik*; song is rollicking and varied series of rich, whistled notes.

WHERE TO FIND: Common to fairly common migrant and summer resident (May–August) in southern valleys in riparian woodlands, open mixed forests, cottonwood stands, and aspen groves. Uncommon to very rare in the northern half of the region.

BEHAVIOUR: Arboreal forager, takes fruits, berries, seeds, and insects. Male and female both sing, sometimes even from the nest or in flight.

DID YOU KNOW? Although male Black-headed and Rose-breasted Grosbeaks look very different, the females are similar in appearance and the two species frequently hybridize where their ranges meet east of the Rockies.

DATE AND LOCATION SEEN: ______________________

____

____

Male
Female

DESCRIPTION: 14 cm. A finch-like bird with **wing-bars**. MALE: **Head and upperparts are bright blue**, **breast is tawny-orange**, belly and wing-bars are white. IMMATURE MALE: More limited blue. FEMALE: Has **plain** grey-brown head and upperparts, **tawny breast**, **narrow white to buffy wing-bars, pale blue-grey rump**. JUVENILE: Resembles female, but breast is finely streaked.

SIMILAR SPECIES: Western Bluebird (p. 309) has rusty-brown back, lacks finch-like bill and wing-bars. Male Indigo Bunting (very rare) darker blue all over; female Indigo Bunting richer brown, lacks bluish rump.

VOICE: Call is sharp *pit*; song is rapid, jumbled, goldfinch-like warble, with many notes given in pairs.

WHERE TO FIND: Common migrant and summer resident (May–September) of brushy areas in low to middle elevations; uncommon to rare north of Williams Lake. Found in dense riparian thickets and shrubby areas of uplands, especially wild rose, snowberry, and mock orange; occasionally in logging clearcuts.

BEHAVIOUR: Diet is mainly insects and seeds. When foraging, gleans food from foliage, hops along the ground, or flies out to catch aerial prey. Builds nest low in thick shrubs or small trees. Female chooses the nest site and builds the nest.

DID YOU KNOW? No two male Lazuli Buntings have identical songs.

DATE AND LOCATION SEEN: ______________________

____

____

Male
Female

DESCRIPTION: 18 cm. Distinctive medium-sized meadow-dwelling songbird with a short, conical bill. BREEDING MALE: **Black head, wings, tail, and underparts; prominent straw-coloured nape; broad white shoulder patch and white rump**. FEMALE and NON-BREEDING MALE: Underparts yellowish buff, upperparts brown with black streaks on back, flanks, and undertail; wings and tail brown; head is buff with dark stripes through eye and on crown.

SIMILAR SPECIES: Male unmistakable; female Red-winged Blackbird (p. 393) resembles female Bobolink but is darker with heavily streaked breast, has longer bill.

VOICE: Call is low *chuk*; song is long, bubbly series of warbling notes.

WHERE TO FIND: Rare to locally common summer resident (May–September) of wet meadows. Most often seen at north end of Osoyoos Lake, lower Similkameen Valley, Brouse (near Nakusp), and in Creston Valley.

BEHAVIOUR: Forages for seeds and insects on the ground or while perched on vegetation. Males are conspicuous, either singing from exposed perches or while making display flights over meadows. Nests colonially in widely scattered locations. Males moult out of bright plumage in late summer and then resemble females and immatures.

DID YOU KNOW? Bobolinks are extraordinary long-distance migrants, travelling thousands of miles from their breeding areas in Canada to wintering areas in southern South America.

DATE AND LOCATION SEEN: ______________________

____

____

Male

Female

DESCRIPTION: 22 cm. Familiar dark-eyed blackbird of wetlands. Male is **black** all over, with **bright red shoulder patch** bordered behind by creamy yellow. Female is somewhat sparrow-like: dark brown, heavily streaked above and below, with buffy eyebrow and throat, reddish-brown tint to wings and back.

SIMILAR SPECIES: Brewer's Blackbird (p. 399) is unstreaked, has pale yellow eyes, and lacks shoulder patches.

VOICE: Calls include a sharp *chek* and *tew*; familiar song is musical *cong-ka-REEE.*

WHERE TO FIND: Common resident of marshes and riparian areas throughout region (February–October); local winter resident in agricultural areas, especially around cattle feedlots and landfills.

BEHAVIOUR: Forages for seeds, insects; travels widely to feed in fields and grasslands. Nests singly or colonially in marshes with tall emergent vegetation, usually in bulrushes.

DID YOU KNOW? Male Red-winged Blackbirds are often polygamous, with harems of up to 15 females living in their territories.

DATE AND LOCATION SEEN: ______________________

____

____

DESCRIPTION: 24 cm. **Stocky and short-tailed** bird of open areas with a long, pointed bill. Cryptic grey-brown above; head has bold stripes. **Bright yellow below with black V on breast** and streaked white sides. Tail is bordered with white. Winter birds and immatures are less boldly marked.

SIMILAR SPECIES: Distinctive.

VOICE: Diverse calls; common ones include a harsh *chuck* and dry rattle; song is a loud, musical, bubbly burst of flutelike whistles.

WHERE TO FIND: Common migrant (February–April, August–October) and summer resident of meadows, pastures, and rangeland, rare north of Quesnel. Rare and local in winter.

BEHAVIOUR: Seen in pairs or small groups in open country, foraging for insects and seeds. Walks on ground, flicking open white-edged tail. Males sing from atop shrubs, boulders, fence posts, or other high perches.

DID YOU KNOW? Western Meadowlark is nearly identical to Eastern Meadowlark, but the two species have very different songs.

DATE AND LOCATION SEEN: ______________________

____

____

Male
Female

Yellow-headed Blackbird

Xanthocephalus xanthocephalus

DESCRIPTION: 24 cm (male)/22 cm (female). Large and distinctive marsh blackbird. MALE: **Black body** contrasts with **bright yellow head**, **neck**, **and breast**; has large **white wing patch**; vent area is yellow. FEMALE: Dark brown with dingy yellow on face, neck, and breast; vent area is yellow. IMMATURE: Faded version of adult male or female.

SIMILAR SPECIES: All other blackbirds lack yellow in plumage.

VOICE: Call is low, rich *k-ruk*; song is harsh, unmusical.

WHERE TO FIND: Locally common migrant (April–May, July–September) and summer resident of deep bulrush marshes, uncommon and local north of Quesnel.

BEHAVIOUR: Forages on aquatic insects, grains, and seeds. Although territorial around nest site, often joins large multi-species blackbird flocks feeding in pastures or farm fields near the nesting area. Male displays by singing from elevated perches, spreading wings and tail, and holding bill pointed upward. Nests colonially in marsh vegetation, always over water. Nomadic after breeding season; flocks forage widely over agricultural fields, meadows, and other open areas. Roosts nightly with other blackbirds in marshes.

DID YOU KNOW? Yellow-headed Blackbirds often nest near Red-winged Blackbirds in marshes, but usually occupy the portions of the marsh with deeper water and emergent vegetation.

DATE AND LOCATION SEEN: ______________________

____

____

Brewer's Blackbird
Male

Brewer's Blackbird
Female

Rusty Blackbird
Male

Rusty Blackbird
Female Winter

DESCRIPTION: 23 cm/32 cm. BREWER'S: Common, conspicuous blackbird with fairly short, pointed bill, and medium-long tail. Male is **shiny black** all over, with iridescent green and purple highlights; **pale yellow eyes**. Female is **solidly dull grey-brown** with dark eyes. RUSTY: Very similar to Brewer's; male is **dull black**, female has **pale eye**. In winter, both sexes have extensive rusty feathering, especially on head and wings.

SIMILAR SPECIES: Smaller Brown-headed Cowbird (p. 401) has smaller, thicker bill, and shorter tail. Immature European Starling (p. 327) has longer bill, and shorter tail. Common Grackle (rare) is much larger with longer tail.

VOICE: BREWER'S: Call is high, sharp *check*; song is high *k-squeesh*. RUSTY: Call is similar to Brewer's but softer; song is a soft, gurgling *ksh-leee*.

WHERE TO FIND: BREWER'S: Common migrant (March-May, September-November) and summer resident of open agricultural areas, residential neighbourhoods, and grasslands. Uncommon in winter; usually around cattle feedlots. RUSTY: Uncommon and local breeder around plateau lakes in northern and subalpine forests; occasionally seen with Brewer's in winter.

BEHAVIOUR: Males deliver songs while fluffing plumage and spreading tail. BREWER'S: Forage on the ground in small flocks mainly for insects and seeds, often in residential areas. Nest in colonies in a wide variety of shrubs or trees, especially columnar cedars.

DID YOU KNOW? Rusty Blackbird populations have declined by over 90 percent in the past 30 years.

DATE AND LOCATION SEEN: ______________________

____

____

Male
Female

DESCRIPTION: 19 cm. **Small**, **short-tailed blackbird** with **dark eyes** and a **stubby**, **finch-like bill**. MALE: Black all over, with a **dark brown head**. FEMALE: Plain grey-brown. Juvenile like female with indistinct streaking and spotting.

SIMILAR SPECIES: Brewer's Blackbird (p. 399) has thinner bill, longer tail; male has pale eyes and shiny black head, female is sootier.

VOICE: Calls include sharp rattle and high flight whistles; song is gurgling *glug-glug-gleeee,* delivered with bowed head and partially spread wings and tail.

WHERE TO FIND: Common migrant (April–May, July–September) and summer resident of riparian woodlands and other open areas with scattered trees. Frequents agricultural areas, but avoids dense coniferous forests. After breeding season, joins mixed blackbird species migratory flocks. Very rare in winter, occasionally persists among mixed blackbird flocks at cattle feedlots.

BEHAVIOUR: Forages mainly on the ground for seeds and insects. Breeding males display and chase females. As brood parasites, females lay eggs in the nests of other songbirds that then raise the cowbird fledglings. Highly gregarious in all seasons.

DID YOU KNOW? In the Okanagan Valley, the Warbling Vireo is the most common host for cowbird eggs and young, with 79 percent of its nests parasitized.

DATE AND LOCATION SEEN: ______________________

____

____

Male
Female

DESCRIPTION: 23 cm. Medium-sized slender bird with long tail, dark and tapered sharp bill. ADULT MALE: **Bright orange** or yellow-orange on underparts, rump, and face**. Black crown**, eye-line, and stripe on chin. **Large white patches on wings**. **Tail** is **orange-yellow with black centre and tip.** FEMALE: Has grey back, pale greyish-white belly. Head and breast are yellow-orange. Rump and tail are dull yellowish. IMMATURE MALE: Resembles female, but with black chin and eye-line.

SIMILAR SPECIES: Male Black-headed Grosbeak (p. 387) has very thick bill and different plumage pattern. Female Western Tanager (p. 357) has dark tail and thicker, yellowish bill.

VOICE: Call is harsh *scheek*; song is rollicking *chik-chicky-tew-tew.*

WHERE TO FIND: Common migrant (April–May, August–September) and summer resident of lowland and foothill riparian woodlands and residential deciduous groves north to Williams Lake.

BEHAVIOUR: Forages for insects and fruit within the foliage of broad-leafed trees, especially cottonwoods and willows. Builds sturdy, pendulous basket-shaped nests that hang from small deciduous tree branches. Male loudly and aggressively defends territory and usually departs from nesting area long before female and young. Readily forages for nectar at hummingbird feeders.

DID YOU KNOW? Orioles occasionally construct their nests with green plastic Easter basket "grass," monofilament fishing line, or bailing twine, and will readily use suitable material provided for them, such as short lengths of yarn or twine.

DATE AND LOCATION SEEN: ______________________

____

____

Coast
Interior

DESCRIPTION: 16 cm. A **cinnamon-brown** ground finch with a **grey head**, black bill (yellow in winter), **black forehead and throat. Belly, rump, and wings are washed with pink**. Females are paler. Birds nesting in Coast Mountains have more extensive grey on head.

SIMILAR SPECIES: Similar finches lack grey on their heads and pink in their wings. Ground-feeding behaviour is usually distinctive.

VOICE: Call a soft, low *cheew*.

WHERE TO FIND: Flocks move to lower elevations in winter. Uncommon to rare and local summer resident of rocky alpine areas, usually those with permanent snowfields; rare winter resident in foothills and valleys.

BEHAVIOUR: Diet is mostly insects and seeds gleaned from bare ground or snow.

DID YOU KNOW? Gray-crowned Rosy-Finches sometimes roost in Cliff Swallow nests in winter.

DATE AND LOCATION SEEN: ______________________

____

____

Male
Female

DESCRIPTION: 23 cm. Large, round-headed boreal finch with dark grey wings and **two bold white wing-bars**. **Tail is long**, **bill is short** and **rounded**. MALE: Has **rose-coloured upperparts**; underparts are variably grey and rose. FEMALE: Grey all over with a variable wash of olive on head and upperparts.

SIMILAR SPECIES: Smaller White-winged Crossbill (p. 413) has a longer, crossed bill.

VOICE: Call is musical *pleedle-eet*; song is clear, distinct finch-type warble.

WHERE TO FIND: Uncommon resident of subalpine forests. Generally common in winter on northern plateaus, uncommon to rare in winter (November–March) in southern valleys, where numbers are unpredictable from year to year.

BEHAVIOUR: Forages on the ground, in trees, in shrubs, and in the air. Diet is mainly buds, seeds, fruits, berries, and some insects. In winter typically seen in small flocks. Occasionally makes short, downslope migrations in winter.

DID YOU KNOW? Pine Grosbeaks are renowned for their quietness, slow movements, and apparent lack of fear of humans. Many feeding flocks likely go unnoticed by birders because they seldom flush or become agitated when approached by people.

DATE AND LOCATION SEEN: ____________________

____

____

Cassin's Finch
Male
Cassin's Finch
Female
Purple Finch
Male
Purple Finch
Female

DESCRIPTION: 16 cm/15 cm. Forest finches with stout bills and **notched tails**. CASSIN'S: Adult male has **scarlet crown;** face, throat, breast, and rump washed with **pale pink**; distinct **back streaks**. Female is greyish-brown with fine black streaks above, **short**, **crisp brownish streaks** on white below **including undertail coverts**; head brown with indistinct whitish eyebrow and cheek patch. PURPLE: Adult male has **raspberry-red head**, **breast**, **and rump**. Brown back and wings pinkish; blurry streaks on sides. Female's head has dark ear patch and crown, indistinct whitish eyebrow and whisker stripe; **blurry brown stripes below, undertail coverts white**; olive-brown back with blurry streaks.

SIMILAR SPECIES: Male House Finch (p. 411) has smaller bill and head, brownish crown, longer tail, and more extensive streaking on belly and flanks. Female House Finch lacks patterned face.

VOICE: CASSIN'S: Call is musical *tr-dlip*. PURPLE: Call is sharp *pik*: both species give descending *whee-oo* call. Songs are rapid warbles.

WHERE TO FIND: CASSIN'S: Common summer resident (March–September) of open, dry coniferous forests in southern half of region, rare to common in winter depending on ponderosa pine seed crop. PURPLE: Uncommon to common summer resident of moist forests and residential areas in northern half of region.

BEHAVIOUR: Both forage for seeds, buds, and some insects. Small flocks in the fall make seasonal movements tied to food availability.

DID YOU KNOW? Both are accomplished mimics—especially Cassin's—often incorporating phrases of other bird sounds into their songs.

DATE AND LOCATION SEEN: ______________________

____

____

Male

Female

DESCRIPTION: 15 cm. Common and familiar songbird with a **short, rounded bill** and long, slightly notched tail. MALE: Variably **red to orange-red,** sometimes even yellow on **forehead**, **eye-stripe**, throat, breast, and rump; **sides and belly have long**, **distinct streaks, crown brownish**. FEMALE: Grey-brown overall, with **long grey-brown blurry streaks below**. **Head is relatively plain and unpatterned**.

SIMILAR SPECIES: Male Cassin's and Purple Finches (p. 409) lack distinct streaks on underparts, have larger, red-crowned heads and shorter tails; females have strong facial patterns.

VOICE: Calls include variety of bright, inflected *chirp* notes. Song is cheery, musical warble, descending slightly and ending with long, burry note.

WHERE TO FIND: A species of human habitats, both urban and rural. Common resident of low-elevation residential areas, farmlands, and pastures. Uncommon and more local in northern communities of region (but population is increasing), common in southern valleys.

BEHAVIOUR: Abundant and unwary, often nesting in planters, on porches, and under eaves. Feeds on seeds and buds; commonly visits seed feeders. Often forms flocks in non-breeding season.

DID YOU KNOW? The red coloration of male House Finches is derived from pigments called carotenoids in their food. The more pigment the male ingests, the redder he becomes. Female House Finches select the reddest males available as breeding partners, perhaps because these males are seemingly the healthiest.

DATE AND LOCATION SEEN: ____________________

Red Crossbill
Male
Red Crossbill
Female
White-winged Crossbill
Male
White-winged Crossbill
Female

DESCRIPTION: 16 cm/16.5 cm. RED: Stocky forest finch with relatively large head; **heavy bill with crossed tips**, **dark wings**, dark notched tail. Typical **adult male** is **brick-red**, **female** is **dull olive**, and juvenile is greyish-brown and heavily streaked. WHITE-WINGED: Medium-sized boreal forest finch that has **dark wings with bold white wing-bars**, **slender bill with crossed tips**, and dark notched tail. **Adult male** is **pinkish-red**, flanks greyish. **Female** is **olive-grey**, indistinctly streaked on flanks. Juvenile is brown and heavily streaked. Immature males of both species duller.

SIMILAR SPECIES: Larger Pine Grosbeak (p. 407) lacks crossed bill tips. Pine Siskin (p. 415) lacks bold wing-bars and crossed bill tips.

VOICE: RED: Flight call is *kip-kip-kip*; song is variable series of short notes, warbles. WHITE-WINGED: Call is *chut-chut-chut*; distinctive song is long series of canary-like trills.

WHERE TO FIND: RED: Common to uncommon, nomadic resident of mature coniferous forests. WHITE-WINGED: Common to rare, highly nomadic resident of mature spruce forests.

BEHAVIOUR: Both species form foraging flocks. Usually feed in tall conifer trees, prying open cones for seed. Both also feed on other seeds, buds, insects, and minerals from soil. Opportunistic wandering breeders, they nest wherever and whenever they find sufficiently large cone seed crops.

DID YOU KNOW? Crossbills often breed in midwinter if conifer seed crops are abundant.

DATE AND LOCATION SEEN: ____________________

Pine Siskin
Common Redpoll

Pine Siskin/Common Redpoll

Carduelis pinus/Carduelis flammea

DESCRIPTION: 12.5 cm/13 cm. SISKIN: **Small** brown bird with short, **notched tail**, long wings, and **thin, pointed bill**. **Streaked above and below**, with **yellow fringes on wings**. Brightest birds have **broad yellow wing-bars**, **yellow stripe on spread wing**, and yellow wash on breast. REDPOLL: **Small**, streaked brownish above, **white below** with coarse black streaking on flanks. **Forehead is red**, **bill base and throat are black**. Male has **rose-pink breast**.

SIMILAR SPECIES: Larger female House Finch (p. 411) has short, thick bill and lacks yellow plumage. Hoary Redpoll (rare) is very similar to Common Redpoll, but larger, paler; has shorter bill, white rump and undertail.

VOICE: SISKIN: Calls include *sheee-u* and buzzy, rising *zzhreeee*; song is mix of calls and trills. REDPOLL: Call is *chit chit chit*; song is series of trilling, buzzy notes.

WHERE TO FIND: SISKIN: Common resident of forests throughout region, especially moist coniferous forests in Columbia Mountains. After breeding, disperses widely. Generally less common in winter. REDPOLL: Common to rare winter resident (November–March) of coniferous forests; open, brushy areas; and riparian woodlands. Irruptive and unpredictable, winter populations often vary on a two-year cycle.

BEHAVIOUR: Diet of both is mainly seeds and insects, especially the small seeds of birches and alders; also readily use bird feeders. Both form post-breeding season flocks.

DID YOU KNOW? Siskins and redpolls are close relatives of the American Goldfinch.

DATE AND LOCATION SEEN: ______________________

____

____

Winter
Male
Female

DESCRIPTION: 13 cm. All plumages have black wings and tail, **prominent wing-bars**, white undertail, **conical bill** (pink in summer). BREEDING: Male: **Bright-yellow** with black forehead. Female: Olive above, yellow below. NON-BREEDING: Tan above, grey below, yellow on throat and "shoulder" of male.

SIMILAR SPECIES: Female Lazuli Bunting (p. 389) lacks white patches on wings and tail.

VOICE: Flight call is *yip-yip*; song is high, musical chattering series.

WHERE TO FIND: Common resident of riparian woodlands, residential areas, and farmland in southern valleys, rare north of Quesnel. In winter concentrates around feeders and weedy fields.

BEHAVIOUR: Forages for seeds and visits backyard feeders, breeds in loose colonial groups, and defends territories near nests. After breeding, they congregate in nomadic flocks.

DID YOU KNOW? American Goldfinches are very late nesters, delaying their breeding until after thistles have produced seed. Thistles provide an important food source for this species as well as material for lining their nests.

DATE AND LOCATION SEEN: ______________________________

____

____

Male

Female

DESCRIPTION: 20 cm. Stocky, short-tailed finch with a **massive head and conical**, **pale greenish-yellow bill**, black wings with **large white wing patches**, and a black tail. MALE: Dark brownish head with **bold yellow eyebrow**; dark brown head and breast fade to yellow on the back and belly. FEMALE: Brownish-grey above, grey below. Juveniles similar to adults but have dusky bills.

SIMILAR SPECIES: Black-headed Grosbeak (p. 387) lacks the yellow eyebrow of the Evening male and the unpatterned head of the female.

VOICE: Calls include high, bell-like *kleer* and high, whistled *teew* notes in flight.

WHERE TO FIND: Fairly common summer resident of mid- to high-elevation coniferous forests. Moves downslope in fall and winters in lower elevation forests, riparian woodlands, and residential areas. Somewhat nomadic; many leave the region in years of poor food supplies.

BEHAVIOUR: Wanders widely; forages for a variety of seeds, buds, fruits, and insects. Typically feeds at the tops and outer branches of trees. Regularly visits bird feeders.

DID YOU KNOW? Although they are known as seed eaters, Evening Grosbeaks are attracted to spruce budworm outbreaks, where they consume huge quantities of caterpillars. Their populations rose significantly from the 1960s through the 1990s as budworm populations boomed across Canada, then declined precipitiously from 1995 to 2005 as the budworm outbreaks disappeared.

DATE AND LOCATION SEEN: ______________________

____

____

Female

DESCRIPTION: 16 cm. Chunky, familiar, introduced sparrow with a stout bill. MALE: Has **black bib** (somewhat obscured by grey feather tips in fall, winter), **grey crown**, pale grey cheeks, **rufous neck sides** and rufous areas on striped back and wings; prominent white wing-bars. Bill is black in breeding season, otherwise yellowish. FEMALE: Dingy grey-brown with tan and brown back stripes; has broad, creamy eyebrow and dull yellowish bill.

SIMILAR SPECIES: Our native sparrows are slimmer, have shorter and more sharply pointed bills, and differ in face pattern.

VOICE: Calls are frequent *chirp* or *cheep* notes; song is monotonous series of call notes.

WHERE TO FIND: Common resident of human-modified areas, usually agricultural and residential areas.

BEHAVIOUR: Picks seeds, grains, crumbs, or insects from the ground. Forms small nesting colonies. Nest is a ball of dried vegetation mixed with feathers and other detritus placed in cavities or crevices of trees, structures, or buildings. Flocks regularly visit bird feeders.

DID YOU KNOW? House Sparrows were first introduced to North America in 1850, but did not reach some portions of our region for another 50 years or so.

DATE AND LOCATION SEEN: ______________________

____

____

Photographer Credits

The letter following the page numbers refer to the position of the photograph on that page (T = top, B = bottom, L= left, R = right, N = inset).

Ted Ardley 25, 33B, 35T, 103, 145TR, 161BL, 215BL, 217T, 219B, 219T, 241T, 257T, 281, 299, 301, 303, 305, 307B, 307T, 311, 317, 343B, 361, 363T, 379B, 399BL, 417B, 417T; Christian Arturo 243B; Jack Bowling 107TR, 345BR, 381TL; Richard Cannings 75BL, 181, 273, 335, 385TL, 385TR, 409TR; Steve Cannings 161TR, 199, 243T, 247B, 319B, 357B, 383TL; Don Cecile 47BL, 47BR, 137B, 145B, 147, 149T, 151BR, 151TL, 157B, 161TL, 163B, 165TR, 165TL, 185, 251B, 371T, 379TL, 385BR, 397T; Alistair Fraser 49T, 93, 235B, 235T, 101, 133T; Jared Hobbs 187, 191, 195, 203B, 203T, 225B, 225T, 231, 263, 325, 331TL, 365B; Ralph Hocken 51T, 53BL, 53BR, 53TL, 53TR, 55BL, 55BR, 55TL, 55TR, 63BL, 63BR, 63TL, 63TR, 69T, 83N, 85T, 89TL, 97B, 97T, 111BL, 111TL, 117T, 131B, 131T, 149B, 151TR, 159BL, 159BR, 173B, 221T, 239B, 259B, 259T, 315, 321B, 321T, 329, 333BL, 337T, 341TL, 341TR, 349B, 351T, 409BL, 413TL, 413TR; Douglas Leighton 205T, 209, 247T; Derick C. MacDonald 65T; Bob McKay 75TR, 77B, 107TL, 111TR, 115BL, 137T, 177B, 207T, 239T, 269, 285T, 331TR, 341BR, 357T, 367, 397B, 399BR; Tom Middleton 29N, 145TL; Laure Wilson Neish 41B, 45B, 69B, 81B, 91B, 139, 153, 163T, 177T, 207TN, 213, 229TR, 245B, 249, 261T, 265, 267, 269N, 275N, 277, 283, 295, 297B, 309BR, 309TL, 309TR, 331B, 333BR, 337B, 347, 351B, 353B, 369, 373, 375, 377, 379TR, 381TR, 383BL, 383TR, 389B, 395, 401B, 401T, 403B, 403T, 407B, 409TL, 411T, 419B, 421B, 421T; John Reaume 399TL; Gerald Romanchuk 27, 39TR, 73, 77BN, 89TR, 107BL, 109B, 111BR, 113B, 113T, 115BR, 115T, 119B, 123T, 123TN, 159T, 171BL, 171BR, 171TL, 171TR, 173T, 233B, 233T, 235N, 241B, 245T, 271, 279, 313, 333TL, 333TR, 339B, 341BL, 345TL, 345TR, 355, 363B, 365T, 371B, 381BL, 381BR, 383BR, 385BL, 405B, 413BL, 413BR; Ian Routley 35B, 37TL, 43B, 43T, 45T, 59B, 61B, 61T,

65T, 75TL, 83B, 83T, 87T, 117B, 121TL, 125B, 135B, 135T, 183, 189, 201, 207B, 215TL, 217B, 223, 229BL, 237, 251T, 253B, 253T, 257B, 285B, 287B, 289, 291F, 293, 309BL, 323, 343T, 349T, 389T, 405T, 419T; Michael G. Shepard 161BR, 165BL, 165BR, 167B, 167T, 209N, 215BR; Tony Beck/VIREO 211F; Wayne C. Weber 51B, 51BN, 89BR, 175T, 319T; Bruce Whittington, 175B; Mike Yip 39BR, 85B, 89BL, 91T, 121TR, 125T, 155, 221B, 255, 353T.

iStock photos from: Carlos Arranz 41T; Norman Bateman 39TL, 227B, Arpad Benedek 151BL; Dennys Bisogno 37TR; Robert Blanchard 79T, 87B, 95N, 129; Inga Brennan 121B, 179; Karel Broz 387B; Steve Byland 327T; Jason Cheever 287T, 359B; Dmitry Deshevykh 157T; Jason Doucette 31B, 99; Elemental Imaging 27N; Sonja Fagnan 31N; James Figlar 345BL; Judy Foldetta 39BL; Teresa Gueck 133B; Robert Hambley 399TR; Lee Horn 119T; Andrew Howe 35N, 415T; Robert Koopmans 71; Frank Leung 37BL, 47TR, 57T, 59TL, 59TR, 67T. 141B, 193, 227T, 275, 387T, 391B, 393B, 393T; Bruce MacQueen 205B; James Metcalf 51TN; Kevin Miller 29, 415B; Laure Neish 31N, 31T, 49B, 57B, 81T, 127, 141T, 407T, 411B, 417N; David Parsons 297T, 359T; Al Parker 75BR; Rich Phalin 143, 169, 261B, 327B, 391T; John Pitcher 107BR, 123BN; Bill Raboin 105, 229BR, 229TL; Philip Robertson 79B, 95; Richard Rodvold 123B, 215TR; Willi Schmitz 327N; William Sherman 47TL; Bill Stamatis 103N; Michael Stubblefield 109T; Paul Tessier 77T, 197, 339T; Ronnie Wilson 409 BR; Dan Wood 33T; xflatcoater 67B.

Acknowledgements

Creating a bird identification guide is a significant undertaking and would not be possible without the contribution of many local birders. Cathy Antoniazzi, Nancy Krueger, Phil Ranson, and Chris Siddle generously reviewed the Species Accounts.

I owe a great debt to the many photographers who provided photographs for this book, consistently meeting the challenge of capturing a bird's key field marks in photographs of high technical and artistic merit. Their names are listed on pages 422–423. In particular, Ralph Hocken, Laure Wilson Neish, Gerald Romanchuk, and Ian Routley spent many hours searching for just the right images. Special thanks to Laure Neish and Gaye Horn for the cover shots.

A number of contributors who aided in the publication of a related US book, *Birds of the Inland Northwest and Northern Rockies*, again are recognized, in particular the authors Harry Nehls, Mike Denny, and Dave Trochlell. Their contributions have been integral to *Birds of Interior BC and the Rockies*.

Also, thanks to Darlene Nickull for the map of the region, and to Eric Kraig for his bird drawings. Julia Cannings cropped the images in the Common Local Birds section.

The success of this guide is the success of all those who have contributed to it. Their participation is sincerely appreciated.

Index/Checklist of Birds of Interior British Columbia and the Rockies

Use this checklist to keep a record of the birds you have seen. The main Species Account page is shown in **bold**.

Other Species Seen

☐ ______________________ ☐ ______________________

☐ ______________________ ☐ ______________________

☐ ______________________ ☐ ______________________

☐ ______________________ ☐ ______________________

☐ ______________________ ☐ ______________________

☐ ______________________ ☐ ______________________

☐ ______________________ ☐ ______________________

☐ ______________________ ☐ ______________________

☐ ______________________ ☐ ______________________

☐ ______________________ ☐ ______________________